WOK COOKERY

COOKSHOP

— WOK —

COOKERY

Cover photograph by Chris Crofton
Inside photography by John Lee

Front cover shows Jambalaya (page 53)
Title page shows Cidered Haddock (page 16)
and Turkey in the Grass (page 26)

Published on behalf of
The Boots Company plc, Nottingham
by Hamlyn Publishing,
a division of The Hamlyn Publishing Group Ltd,
Bridge House, London Road, Twickenham, Middlesex, England

© Copyright Hamlyn Publishing 1985
Fourth impression 1987

First published under the title
Cooking with a Wok

ISBN 0 600 32550 4

Set in 10 on 11pt Monophoto Gill Sans
by Servis Filmsetting Ltd, Manchester

Printed in Italy

Contents

Useful Facts & Figures

Notes on metrication

In this book quantities are given in metric and Imperial measures. Exact conversion from Imperial to metric measures does not usually give very convenient working quantities and so the metric measures have been rounded off into units of 25 grams. The table below shows the recommended equivalents.

Ounces	Approx g to nearest whole figure	Recommended conversion to nearest unit of 25
1	28	25
2	57	50
3	85	75
4	113	100
5	142	150
6	170	175
7	198	200
8	227	225
9	255	250
10	283	275
11	312	300
12	340	350
13	368	375
14	396	400
15	425	425
16 (1 lb)	454	450
17	482	475
18	510	500
19	539	550
20 (1¼ lb)	567	575

Note: When converting quantities over 20 oz first add the appropriate figures in the centre column, then adjust to the nearest unit of 25. As a general guide, 1 kg (1000 g) equals 2.2 lb or about 2 lb 3 oz. This method of conversion gives good results in nearly all cases, although in certain pastry and cake recipes a more accurate conversion is necessary to produce a balanced recipe.

Liquid measures The millilitre has been used in this book and the following table gives a few examples.

Imperial	Approx ml to nearest whole figure	Recommended ml
¼ pint	142	150 ml
½ pint	283	300 ml
¾ pint	425	450 ml
1 pint	567	600 ml
1½ pint	851	900 ml
1¾ pints	992	1000 ml (1 litre)

Spoon measures All spoon measures given in this book are level unless otherwise stated.

Can sizes At present, cans are marked with the exact (usually to the nearest whole number) metric equivalent of the Imperial weight of the contents, so we have followed this practice when giving can sizes.

Oven temperatures

The table below gives recommended equivalents.

	°C	°F	Gas
Very cool	110	225	¼
	120	250	½
Cool	140	275	1
	150	300	2
Moderate	160	325	3
	180	350	4
Moderately hot	190	375	5
	200	400	6
Hot	220	425	7
	230	450	8
Very hot	240	475	9

Note: *When making any of the recipes in this book, only follow one set of measures as they are not interchangeable.*

Clockwise, from the top: *stainless steel wok, non-stick coated wok, electric wok, carbon steel wok and a selection of useful accessories*

Introduction

Types of wok available

The traditional and most common type of wok is that made from carbon or tempered steel. In addition, stainless steel woks and those with a non-stick coating are also available. Plug-in electric ones are made of carbon steel or they can be non-stick. Generally, the wok is completely curved, but there are some which have slightly flattened bases and these are particularly useful for electric hobs. Away from the Chinese supermarkets, ethnic shops and specialist cook shops, most woks are sold in kit form complete with a stand, lid, steaming rack and a variety of small accessories. It is important to make sure that your wok has a good lid – well domed and well fitting, and not made of carbon or tempered steel. Look at the type of handles on the wok; some have a pair of metal handles – these will become very hot during cooking – while others have a pair of handles with wooden grips or a single wooden handle, both of which are quite practical. Before you buy a wok think about how often you are going to use it and what cooking techniques you are going to use it for, then look around and decide which type you would prefer. The following notes may be of some help when you are trying to decide, but also read through the notes on accessories before you part with your cash!

Carbon steel or tempered steel wok

This is the traditional type of wok. Made of thin metal a wok like this heats up very quickly and it is very responsive to an increase or decrease in heat. However, without care, this type of wok rusts easily – it needs to be kept oiled and free from damp. Ideally, a carbon steel wok should be used fairly frequently, in which case it is the best type to buy. After extensive use the steel builds up an excellent cooking surface – blackened, and not one which sticks easily. Make sure the lid is either of stainless steel or aluminium; a carbon steel lid presents a permanent rust problem and it can be a great nuisance!

So, if you plan to use your wok all the time, buy one of this type and make a real effort to give it hard use for the first few weeks to build up the cooking surface. But do be honest with yourself and, if you are only going to rummage in the cupboard for your wok on a biennial basis, then go for one of the other types.

Care and storage. New carbon steel woks have a wax coating which has to be removed by scouring the wok in hot soapy water. The wok should be rinsed and thoroughly dried, then seasoned. To do this heat the wok and pour in a little oil, then rub it around the pan with a pad of absorbent kitchen paper. Heat the wok until it is smoking hot, wipe it again and repeat once more. Wipe the outside of the wok with oil too.

After cooking with fat, there is no need to wash the wok – it should be washed as rarely as possible – simply wipe it out with plenty of absorbent kitchen paper and use salt as a scouring agent, with a little fresh oil to clean the surface. If you have prepared a saucy dish or one which has stuck slightly, then wash the wok in soapy water and re-season it. This type of wok is best kept hanging in a dry, well-ventilated place.

Stainless steel wok

This does not have the same rust problems as a carbon steel wok but it does not reach as high a temperature and it is not as responsive to temperature changes. It is also more prone to damage from scratching than the carbon steel type. However, some stainless steel woks have a slightly flattened base which makes them useful for electric rings and elminates the necessity for a stand.

Care and storage. Wash the stainless steel wok in hot soapy water, keeping the cooking surface lightly oiled for best cooking results. A special stainless steel cleaner can be used on a wok and after use the wok can be stored in a cupboard with no fear of rusting.

Non-stick coated wok

Again, this type of wok does not rust and most have a slightly flattened base. They do not heat up as quickly as the carbon steel woks and they are not quite as responsive to heat changes, but they do have their advantages in that they are very easy to clean and, depending on the quality of the coating, they do not stick at all. Remember not to use metal utensils on non-stick surfaces. This type of wok is only as good as the coating on the cooking surface.

Care and storage. Always follow the manufacturer's instructions for the care of non-stick utensils. This usually involves washing the wok in hot soapy water; it should never be scoured during cleaning.

Electric wok
I was most impressed with the electric wok which I tested – it was an attractive, efficient appliance. The notes on the non-stick wok also apply to an electric wok, which has a non-stick coating. An electric wok is, in fact, an independent work-top cooker which is ideal for the bedsit cook with no other cooking facilities. Not only can complete meals be cooked in the wok, but they can also be served from it. I even took mine out into the garden on an extension lead to add a new dimension to barbecued food!

Look for an appliance with a detachable lead (like an electric kettle) and check the instructions to see whether the wok can be immersed in water for cleaning.

Care and storage. Always follow the manufacturer's instructions for cleaning electrical appliances. This type of wok is best kept out on the work top in the kitchen.

Accessories
Most woks come complete with a stand to place over the cooker hob. With sloping sides, these metal stands can be used to hold the wok near to the heat source, as required in the case of an electric ring, or it can be turned over to keep the wok above a gas flame. These stands can also be purchased separately.

Second only in importance to the stand is the lid. This is the other basic accessory needed for braising and steaming in the wok. Make sure that the lid fits well and that it has a wooden knob or one which will not become too hot when in use. A steaming rack is also important for cooking in the wok and it is usually included in wok kits; if not, one can be bought separately or a round, suitably sized cake rack can be used instead.

A variety of small accessories, such as ladles and spoons for tossing, turning, stirring and draining foods, is also available. These are not essential – if you have a reasonably well-equipped kitchen then you do not need them – but they do add to the fun of cooking in your wok.

Bamboo steamers are very useful because they can be rested over the wok and several layers can be stacked one on top of another, to cook and reheat a selection of dishes at the same time. If you are going to buy a set, choose those with a reasonably large diameter so that you can fit large dishes inside.

In addition, chopsticks and small bowls are useful if you are planning to prepare Chinese food. These are sometimes included in wok kits but are also readily available elsewhere.

Cooking techniques
Wok cooking is usually quite fast, so prepare all the ingredients in advance and you won't have any problems. If you follow the recipe instructions fairly closely you will find that all the foods are prepared in the order which is necessary for successful cooking. Once you've used your wok for a while you will become accustomed to the speed with which it heats up and you will know how long in advance to turn on the heat.

Stir frying. This is the method most commonly associated with wok cooking and a traditional type of wok is by far the best appliance for this rapid food frying. The hot deep sides of the wok provide a large surface area and plenty of depth to sear and toss the food without throwing it out of the pan. It is most important to have all the ingredients ready before you start stir-frying – they should be cut evenly and finely.

Shallow frying. You can use your wok for most of the shallow frying normally carried out in a frying pan. However it is sometimes better to use an ordinary frying pan – for example, several eggs cannot be fried together in the wok!

Deep frying. Because of its shape the wok is not ideal for deep frying loads of chips and *it should not be used as a substitute for the western form of deep frying pan.* However, it is useful for frying small individual items of food as the well of the wok gives a good depth of fat even if only a small amount is used.

Braising. The wok, with its domed lid, is ideal for braising foods, both large and small. The dish remains moist and quite large quantities can be cooked in this way – even whole birds can be braised in the wok.

Steaming. The wok makes a wonderful steamer. With the steaming rack in place, puddings, fish, meat and rice can be steamed. The domed lid allows plenty of room for the food dishes or basins to stand on the rack and it also helps the steam to condense quickly during cooking. For long steaming the water does have to be topped up, but for shorter steaming times the moisture which runs back down into the wok is usually sufficient.

Soups

All soups rely on the quality of the cooking liquid for their eventual flavour and so the basic stock recipe given here can be used as the foundation of many interesting Oriental soups. The soup should be served in small bowls with Chinese porcelain spoons to scoop it up.

RICH CHICKEN STOCK

MAKES 900 ml / 1½ pints

2 chicken joints
225 g / 8 oz belly of pork (pick out the leanest you can find)
1 large onion
large bay leaf
6 peppercorns
about 1.4 litres / 2½ pints water

Place the chicken joints in the wok. Cut the pork into cubes and cut the onion into chunks, then place both in the wok with the chicken. Add the bay leaf and peppercorns and pour in the water, adding a little extra, if necessary, just to cover the meats. Bring to the boil and skim off any scum which rises to the surface. Put the lid on the wok and reduce the heat so that the stock simmers steadily. Cook for an hour.

Lift the chicken joints out of the stock and cut all the meat off. Chop this and reserve for use in the soup, or for another purpose. Remove and discard the onion, pork and bay leaf, then strain the stock through a piece of fine muslin or a coffee filter paper. If the stock looks greasy, then chill it thoroughly and skim off the fat. The stock is now ready for use, but remember that it is not seasoned.

A simple chicken soup can be prepared by returning the chopped chicken to the stock and adding seasoning to taste. Heat through and sprinkle some chopped parsley into the light broth. This is excellent for slimmers.

The stock can be kept in the refrigerator for a few days, or it can be frozen for later use.

EGG DROP SOUP

SERVES 4

This widely known Chinese soup is easily prepared in the wok as it gives a large surface area of soup into which the beaten egg can be swirled. The success of this soup depends on the quality of the stock, so don't cut corners and try to use a cube.

900 ml / 1½ pints Rich Chicken Stock
6 spring onions
2 tablespoons chopped fresh coriander leaves
about 4 tablespoons soy sauce
salt and freshly ground black pepper
2 teaspoons cornflour
1 tablespoon cold water
2 eggs

Prepare the stock according to the recipe instructions, straining it and removing any excess fat if necessary. Stir in the chopped chicken meat. Finely chop the spring onions and mix them with the coriander.

Pour the stock into the wok and heat through, then stir in the soy sauce, tasting the soup as you do so, and add seasoning to taste. The soup will need some pepper but, depending on the strength of the soy sauce, it may not need any salt. Blend the cornflour with the water and stir into the hot soup, then bring to the boil to thicken slightly.

Beat the eggs thoroughly without allowing them to become frothy – the idea is to combine the yolks and whites evenly. Stir the spring onion mixture into the soup, bring to a rapid boil and stir the soup so that it swirls around vigorously in the wok. Immediately turn off the heat and pour in the egg in a slow thin steam. It should set in thin strips.

CHICKEN AND SWEET CORN SOUP

SERVES 4

(Illustrated above)

Serve crisp prawn crackers to complement this soup.

*900 ml/ 1½ pints Rich Chicken Stock
(page 14)
350 g/ 12 oz sweet corn
salt and freshly ground black pepper
2 teaspoons cornflour (optional)
1 tablespoon water (optional)
chopped spring onions to garnish
(optional)*

Prepare the stock according to the recipe instructions, straining it and removing any excess fat if necessary. Pour the stock into the wok and add 225 g/8 oz of the sweet corn. Bring to the boil, add seasoning and simmer for 15 minutes with the lid on the wok. Blend the soup in a liquidiser until smooth, then return it to the wok.

Reheat the soup and decide whether it is thick enough for your liking. If not, blend the cornflour with the water and stir it into the soup, then bring to the boil. Add the remaining sweet corn and the chopped chicken reserved from preparing the stock. Simmer for 5 minutes, then taste and adjust the seasoning before serving, garnished with spring onions if you like.

Fish Dishes

The wok is ideal for cooking fish and seafood because these are foods which taste best when cooked quickly. Whether steamed, braised or fried, wok-cooked fish tastes simply splendid.

STUFFED COD

SERVES 2

(Illustrated opposite)

50 g/2 oz butter
2 sticks celery, chopped
1 small onion, chopped
2 rashers streaky bacon, rind removed and chopped
50 g/2 oz fresh breadcrumbs
salt and freshly ground black pepper
milk
2 cod steaks, bones removed
350 g/12 oz new carrots
bay leaf
300 ml/½ pint dry white wine
150 ml/¼ pint water
2 egg yolks
4 tablespoons double cream
chopped parsley to garnish

Melt the butter in the wok, add the celery, onion and bacon, and cook, stirring continuously until the onion is soft and the bacon cooked. Add to the breadcrumbs, with seasoning, and stir well, add enough milk to bind the ingredients. Divide this stuffing between the cod steaks, placed on buttered foil.

Add the carrots to the wok and throw in the bay leaf, then pour in the wine and water. Stand the steaming rack over the vegetables and heat to boiling point. Reduce the heat. Pack the fish closely in the foil, making sure that the edges are well sealed, and place the package on the steaming rack. Put the lid on the wok and simmer gently for 20 minutes. Transfer the fish to a heated serving dish and, using a draining spoon, lift the carrots out of the liquid. Arrange them round the fish.

Whisk the egg yolks with the cream and stir into the liquid in the wok. Heat very gently without boiling (it will curdle if overheated) then pour it over the fish. Sprinkle with chopped parsley and serve.

CIDERED HADDOCK

SERVES 4

(Illustrated opposite)

The wok is ideal for poaching fillets of larger fish because they do not usually fit into an average frying pan unless they are cut up. This very simple dish is delicious: the tangy cider complements the fish very well. Serve it with boiled rice, creamed or baked potatoes, or buttered new potatoes.

4 medium-sized haddock fillets
1 large onion
1 green pepper
2 carrots
50 g/2 oz butter or
2 tablespoons oil
2 tablespoons plain flour
salt and freshly ground black pepper
600 ml/1 pint dry cider
bay leaf
4 tablespoons chopped parsley
100 g/4 oz sweet corn

Skin the fish fillets (see Paupiettes Florentine, page 18). Thinly slice the onion. Cut the stalk end off the green pepper and remove all the seeds and pith from inside, then slice the green flesh. Thinly slice the carrots.

Melt the butter or heat the oil in the wok and add the onion and green pepper, then fry, turning the slices frequently, until the onion has softened. Stir in the flour and seasoning and cook for a minute, then pour in the cider and add the bay leaf, parsley and carrots. Bring to the boil, reduce the heat so that the sauce simmers and slide the fish into the wok. Put the lid on and cook for 30 minutes. Sprinkle the sweet corn into the wok for the last 5 minutes of cooking time.

Serve immediately, straight from the wok if you like, or carefully transferred to a heated serving platter or dish.

PAUPIETTES FLORENTINE

SERVES 4

(Illustrated above)

Whereas most frying pans are only large enough to cook a few rolls of fish at a time, the wok is big enough to enable eight fillets of plaice to be cooked at once. Combined with a garnish of crisp fried potatoes this dish can be served with either a salad or some lightly boiled French beans or peas.

8 large plaice fillets
salt and freshly ground black pepper
1 (300-g/10.6-oz) packet frozen
chopped spinach, thawed
50 g/2 oz Emmental cheese, grated
freshly grated nutmeg
675 g/1½ lb potatoes
grated rind of 1 lemon
2 tablespoons oil
50 g/2 oz butter
parsley sprigs to garnish (optional)

First skin the fish fillets. Place the fillets on a board, skin side down, and rub your fingers in a little salt. Holding the tail end of each fillet firmly between your salted fingers, use a sharp knife to cut between the skin and the flesh of the fish. Hold the knife at an acute angle to the board and use a slight sawing motion to ease the flesh off the skin without puncturing the skin at all.

Mix the thoroughly drained spinach with the cheese, nutmeg and plenty of salt and pepper. Spread a little of this mixture over each fish fillet and roll them up to enclose the filling. Use wooden cocktail sticks to secure the rolls.

Cut the potatoes into small even dice and mix them with the lemon rind. Heat the oil and butter together in the wok, add the fish rolls and fry them until browned all over. Remove the fish from the pan. Add the potatoes to the fat remaining in the wok and cook over high heat until golden brown all over. Place the steaming rack over the potatoes and reduce the heat under the wok. Arrange the fish on the rack and put the lid on the wok. Cook gently for 15 minutes.

Carefully lift the fish off the rack, then arrange the rolls in a heated serving dish. Spoon the potatoes around the fish and garnish with parsley sprigs, if liked, before serving.

FISH WITH BLACK BEAN SAUCE

SERVES 4

Black bean sauce is a traditional accompaniment to fish and chicken in oriental dishes; it is rich and delicious. Salted black beans are small wrinkled black beans with a pungent, salty taste. They are sold in packets or they are sometimes described as fermented beans and sold in cans; they can be obtained from oriental supermarkets or delicatessen shops.

25 g/ 1 oz fresh root ginger
4 large spring onions
1 large clove garlic
sesame oil
3 tablespoons salted black beans
1 tablespoon lemon juice
2 tablespoons soy sauce
2 teaspoons sugar
150 ml/¼ pint dry sherry
675 g/ 1½ lb white fish fillet, in two thick pieces (for example, cod, haddock or coley)
1 red pepper, cut into fine strips, to garnish

Scrub the ginger, then cut it into very fine strips. Cut the spring onions diagonally into fine strips and chop the garlic. Heat a little oil in the wok and add the ginger and garlic, with the black beans. Stir-fry for a few minutes, then stir in the lemon juice, soy sauce, sugar and sherry.

Skin the fish (see Paupiettes Florentine, page 18) and lay the fillets in the sauce in the wok. Simmer gently for 20 to 25 minutes, by which time the fish should be cooked through. Sprinkle the spring onions over the top of the fish, cook for just a few minutes longer, then transfer to a heated serving dish. Serve immediately, garnished with the red pepper strips.

Note: The black bean sauce can be used as a cooking medium for chicken or prawns. Prepare thin slices of uncooked chicken, or use peeled cooked prawns, and simmer them in the sauce as above.

ORIENTAL FISHBALLS

SERVES 4

Serve this fish and vegetable dish with rice or chow mein noodles to complete the meal.

450 g/ 1 lb white fish
5 tablespoons soy sauce
1 generous tablespoon plain flour
4 dried Chinese mushrooms
1 small onion
2 pieces canned bamboo shoot
450 g/ 1 lb Chinese cabbage
oil for frying
4 tablespoons dry sherry

Skin the fish (see Paupiettes Florentine, page 18) and chop the flesh, removing any bones. Mix the chopped fish with a scant tablespoon of the soy sauce and with the flour, then pound the ingredients thoroughly until they are combined. Take small spoonfuls of the fish mixture and knead it into balls in the palms of your hands.

Place the mushrooms in a small basin and pour on sufficient boiling water to cover. Leave to soak for 20 minutes. Halve and finely slice the onion and finely slice the pieces of bamboo shoot. Shred the cabbage and mix it with the bamboo shoots. Drain the soaked mushrooms and slice them too.

Heat the oil in the wok and add the fishballs, then fry, turning carefully, until golden brown on all sides. Remove them from the wok and drain on absorbent kitchen paper. Add the onion and mushrooms to the oil remaining in the wok and stir-fry for a few minutes, then add the cabbage and bamboo shoots and continue to cook for a minute. Pour in the remaining soy sauce and the sherry. Replace the fishballs on top of the vegetables and put the lid on the wok, then cook over medium heat for 2 to 3 minutes. Serve immediately, straight from the wok if you like.

TROUT WITH COURGETTES

SERVES 2

(Illustrated opposite)

It is possible to cook more than two trout in the wok at the same time, but if they are fairly large they may become slightly curved due to the shape of the wok. If you do want to prepare four fish, then brown the fish two at a time in the wok and arrange them on the steaming rack over the courgettes to finish cooking.

50 g/2 oz butter
2 trout, gutted
4 courgettes
2 tablespoons chopped dill
salt and freshly ground black pepper
Garnish:
lemon wedges
dill sprigs

Melt the butter in the wok and add the trout. Cook until browned on the underside, then carefully turn the fish over and cook until browned on the second side. Meanwhile, slice the courgettes.

Sprinkle the courgettes over the fish in the pan. Allow as many of the slices as possible to sit beside the fish in the wok, then sprinkle the chopped dill over and add a little seasoning. Put the lid on the wok and cook gently for 20 minutes, turning the fish over after 10 minutes' cooking time.

Serve immediately on a warmed serving platter, with the courgettes arranged round the fish, garnished with lemon wedges and dill sprigs.

CRUNCHY-TOPPED COLEY

SERVES 4

(Illustrated opposite)

This is an economical recipe for those useful pre-formed fish steaks which have no skin or bones to worry about. Serve baked potatoes as an accompaniment if you want a substantial meal, or offer a green salad and some crusty bread for a lighter result.

4 coley steaks
salt and freshly ground black pepper
2 tablespoons plain flour
4 slices bread
4 tomatoes
2 sticks celery
50 g/2 oz black olives (optional)
2 cloves garlic
50 g/2 oz butter
2 tablespoons oil
chopped parsley to garnish (optional)

There is no need to defrost the fish steaks: simply sprinkle them with plenty of seasoning and dust them with flour.

Cut the crusts off the bread and cut the slices into neat cubes. Place the tomatoes in a bowl and cover them with boiling water, leave to stand for about 30 seconds, then drain and peel them. Cut the peeled tomatoes into eighths. Thinly slice the celery, and stone the olives if using.

Crush the garlic into the wok and add the butter and oil. Heat gently until the butter melts, then increase the heat and add the cubes of bread. Fry these on all sides until golden, then remove from the wok and drain on absorbent kitchen paper.

Add the fish to the fat remaining in the pan and fry on both sides until golden brown and cooked. Remove from the wok and place on a heated serving dish; keep hot.

Add the celery to the wok and stir over a high heat for a minute. Then add the tomatoes, and the olives if using, and cook for a few minutes more. Taste and adjust the seasoning. Spoon this mixture over the fish in the serving dish and top with the bread croûtons, then sprinkle with chopped parsley and serve immediately.

Alternatively, the fish steaks can be returned to the wok, arranged neatly on the vegetables, topped with croûtons, then garnished for serving straight from the pan.

Poultry Dishes

Poultry is one of the most economical and versatile of foods. You will find that even a whole chicken can be cooked in the wok with moist, tender results. There are recipes for turkey and duck too, so take your pick!

PROVENÇAL CHICKEN

SERVES 4

(Illustrated on page 25)

Serve this simple chicken casserole with boiled or sautéed potatoes, buttered rice or pasta and a salad.

450 g/ I lb tomatoes
50 g/2 oz black olives
3 tablespoons plain flour
salt and freshly ground black pepper
4 chicken joints
3 tablespoons olive oil
2 large cloves garlic
bay leaf
150 ml/¼ pint full-bodied red wine
chopped parsley to garnish

Place the tomatoes in a large bowl and cover with boiling water. Allow them to stand for 30 seconds to a minute, then drain and peel them. Cut the peeled tomatoes into quarters and set aside. Stone the olives and mix them with the tomatoes. Mix the flour with plenty of seasoning and use to coat the chicken joints.

Heat the oil in the wok and crush the garlic into it. Add the chicken joints and fry, turning frequently, until well browned on all sides. Add the bay leaf and pour in the wine, then spoon the tomatoes and olives over the top and bring just to boiling point. Put the lid on the wok and allow the chicken to simmer for 30 to 40 minutes. Sprinkle the parsley over before serving either straight from the wok or transferred to a warmed serving dish.

CHICKEN WITH BROCCOLI

SERVES 4

(Illustrated on page 25)

Here is a light and summery stir-fry dish which is not oriental. Serve it with boiled new potatoes sprinkled with chopped fresh herbs, or with boiled rice.

450 g/ I lb boneless chicken breast
450 g/ I lb broccoli
50 g/2 oz butter
salt and freshly ground black pepper
50 g/2 oz flaked almonds
I tablespoon plain flour
juice of I orange
150 ml/¼ pint dry white wine

Cut the chicken meat into fine strips. Break the broccoli into small florets, cutting through the stalk if necessary and discarding any particularly tough stalks. Melt the butter in the wok and add the chicken strips. Season to taste and cook until they are browned all over, then stir in the almonds and cook until they are also lightly browned.

Sprinkle the flour over the chicken and stir over the heat for a minute. Pour in the orange juice and wine and bring to the boil, then reduce the heat and add the broccoli. Simmer for 2 minutes, or until the broccoli is just tender but still crisp and whole. Taste and adjust the seasoning if necessary and serve immediately.

CHICKEN IN A WOK

SERVES 4

I was very pleasantly surprised when I first cooked a whole chicken in my wok. Not only did the bird cook successfully without the need to top up the liquid several times during cooking, but the result was mouth-watering – tender, very well flavoured and all in just about an hour! There is no need to serve any accompaniments with this dish but some warm Granary bread would go very well if you really do have a hungry crowd on your hands.

1 (1.5-kg/3½-lb) oven-ready chicken
225 g/8 oz carrots
450 g/1 lb potatoes
2 large onions
225 g/8 oz French beans
50 g/2 oz butter
bay leaf
3 sprigs parsley
2 sprigs thyme
sprig of sage
pared rind of ½ lemon
salt and freshly ground black pepper

900 ml/1½ pints dry cider or chicken stock

Trim off the ends of the wings and legs from the chicken. Cut the carrots into chunks and cut the potatoes in half, or quarters if they are very large. Slice the onions fairly thickly and separate the slices into rings. Trim the French beans if they are fresh. Melt the butter in the wok and add the chicken. Fry, turning frequently, until well browned all over. Add the onion rings and cook for a few minutes. While the chicken is browning tie the bay leaf and other herbs into a small bunch with the lemon rind.

Sprinkle a little seasoning over the chicken – add this sparingly at this stage if you are going to use ready-seasoned stock. Add the bouquet garni and pour in the cider or stock. Bring to the boil and put the lid on the wok. Reduce the heat so that the liquid simmers steadily and cook for 30 minutes. Open the wok and add the carrots and potatoes, then bring the liquid back to the boil, regulate the heat so that it simmers again and put the lid back on the wok. Simmer for a further 30 minutes. Add the French beans and cook for 10 minutes, then serve straight from the wok.

SWEET AND SOUR CHICKEN

SERVES 4

1 large green pepper
1 large onion
3 carrots
1 stick celery
3 canned pineapple rings
2 tablespoons soy sauce
2 tablespoons cider vinegar
2 tablespoons dark brown sugar
2 tablespoons concentrated
tomato purée
2 tablespoons dry sherry
1 teaspoon cornflour
2 teaspoons water
4 chicken joints
2 tablespoons plain flour
salt and freshly ground black pepper
2 tablespoons oil

Cut the stalk end off the green pepper, scoop out and discard all the seeds and pith, and cut the flesh into thin slices. Slice the onion, then separate the slices into rings. Cut the carrots and celery into fine strips, and cut the pineapple into small pieces.

In a measuring jug, mix the soy sauce, vinegar, sugar, tomato purée and sherry, then make the mixture up to 250 ml/8 fl oz with water. Stir well to dissolve the sugar. Mix the cornflour with the water and stir this into the sauce. Set aside.

Coat the chicken joints in the flour and sprinkle a little seasoning over them. Heat the oil in the wok and fry the chicken over a medium heat until well browned on all sides. To test if the joints are ready, pierce the thickest part of the joint with a knife – the juices should be clear with no sign of blood. If you are in any doubt as to whether the chicken is cooked, then continue frying the joints over a low to medium heat without letting them become too brown. Remove the chicken pieces from the wok and drain them on absorbent kitchen paper. Set aside and keep hot.

To make the sauce, add the pepper, onion, carrot and celery to the fat left in the wok and stir-fry for 2 minutes. First stir the liquid ingredients in the jug then pour over the vegetables in the wok. Cook, stirring, over a high heat until the sauce boils, then simmer for a minute. Stir in the pineapple and spoon the sauce over the chicken.

Top: *Provençal Chicken*; bottom: *Chicken with Broccoli (both on page 22)*

TURKEY IN THE GRASS

SERVES 4

(Illustrated above)

This is a delicious dish with a very silly title – in fact it should be called 'grass in the turkey' but that sounds particularly unappetising! However, there is grass in the recipe: lemon grass is used to give simple stir-fried turkey flavour and an excellent aroma. Serve with a rice dish.

675 g| 1½ lb boneless turkey breast
3 thick stalks lemon grass
25 g| 1 oz fresh root ginger
50 g| 2 oz butter
1 clove garlic
1 tablespoon rich soy sauce
1 head curly endive
3 spring onions
1 lemon, cut into wedges, to garnish

Cut the turkey into bite-sized cubes. Cut the lemon grass in half lengthways and then cut the strips in half widthways. Slice the ginger and mix it with the lemon grass.

Melt the butter in the wok, crush the garlic into it and add the lemon grass and ginger. Cook, stirring continuously, for a few minutes, then add the turkey and continue stir-frying until the meat has browned all over and is cooked through. Add the soy sauce and cook gently for a few minutes more.

Separate and rinse the leaves of endive, dry them thoroughly, then arrange them on a serving dish. Trim and chop the spring onions and sprinkle them over the endive. Arrange the turkey on top and pour over any juices from the wok. Serve immediately, garnished with the lemon wedges – when served, the juice can be squeezed from these to add zest to the turkey and salad.

PEANUT-COATED TURKEY

SERVES 4

(Illustrated below)

225 g/8 oz salted peanuts
freshly ground black pepper
4 large turkey fillets
4 tablespoons plain flour
I egg, lightly beaten
I tablespoon oil
Garnish:
4 tomatoes
I small onion
chopped parsley

Finely chop the peanuts and season them with a little pepper, then place them on a plate. Dip the turkey fillets first in the flour, then in the beaten egg, and finally in the nuts, pressing them on well.

Heat the oil in the wok, add the turkey fillets and cook, turning once, until golden on both sides and cooked through. Transfer to a heated serving dish and keep hot. Slice the tomatoes and onion and separate the onion slices into rings. Arrange these on top of the turkey fillets and sprinkle the parsley in a neat row down the middle; serve immediately.

ORIENTAL DUCK WITH PINEAPPLE

SERVES 4

(Illustrated on page 29)

I oven-ready duck
1.15 litres/2 pints water
3 tablespoons rich soy sauce
I fresh pineapple
I (227-g/8-oz) can water chestnuts
I bunch spring onions
2 green chillies
sesame oil
I large clove garlic

Cut the duck in half lengthways, using a meat cleaver and poultry scissors. Place the halves in the wok and pour in the water, then add I tablespoon of the soy sauce. Put the lid on the wok and bring to the boil. Reduce the heat so that the liquid simmers steadily and cook for an hour.

While the duck is cooking prepare the remaining ingredients. Trim the leaves off the pineapple and cut off the stalk end. Cut off the peel and cut out all the spines, then slice the fruit in half lengthways and remove the hard core. Cut the pineapple halves into slices and set aside. Drain and slice the water chestnuts and slice the spring onions diagonally. Cut the stalks off the chillies and remove all their seeds, then slice the green part thinly.

At the end of simmering time remove the duck from the stock and set it aside. Pour the stock out of the wok (this should be chilled and the fat skimmed off, then the stock can be used in oriental soups and stews) and wipe out the pan. Grease it with a little sesame oil.

When the duck is cool enough to handle cut all the meat off the bones and slice it into pieces. Heat the wok and add the chillies, crush the garlic into the pan and add the duck. Stir-fry until lightly browned, then add the water chestnuts and pineapple and cook for a few minutes. Stir in the remaining soy sauce and any juice from the fruit, and sprinkle over the spring onions. Cook for a minute before serving straight from the wok.

WUN TUN DUCK

SERVES 4

(Illustrated opposite)

You can either make the wun tuns yourself or you can buy the skins from a Chinese supermarket. The combination of cooked duck, crisp wun tuns and the sweet and sour sauce in this recipe is well worth all the effort. If you intend to serve this for a dinner party, cook the duck and prepare the wun tun dough in advance.

1 oven-ready duck
1.15 litres/2 pints water
4–5 tablespoons soy sauce
4 slices fresh root ginger
1 quantity wun tun dough (page 37)
1 red pepper
1 carrot
1 small onion
1 tablespoon oil
2 tablespoons tomato ketchup
2 tablespoons cider vinegar
2 tablespoons dry sherry
1 tablespoon sugar
900 ml/ 1½ pints oil for deep frying

Trim off the ends of the wings and legs of the duck; cut in half lengthways. Place both pieces in the wok and pour in the water. Add 3 tablespoons of the soy sauce and the ginger and bring to the boil. Reduce the heat so that the liquid simmers steadily and put the lid on the wok. Cook for an hour, checking occasionally that the water has not dried up and turning the duck half-way through the cooking time.

Prepare the wun tun dough and roll it out according to the recipe instructions. Keep it covered while preparing the sauce. Cut the stalk end off the red pepper and remove all the seeds and pith from inside, then halve and thinly slice the flesh. Cut the carrot into very fine strips and halve and thinly slice the onion, separating the pieces into fine strips.

When the duck is cooked, remove it from the wok and drain thoroughly. Leave until cool enough to handle, then cut off all the meat. Discard any fat and cut the meat into strips. Pour off the stock, reserving it for use in soups and stews. Rinse and wipe out the wok, greasing it if necessary.

Add the oil to the wok and heat over a high heat. Fry the strips of duck until browned, then add the pepper, carrot and onion strips and cook quickly over a high heat. Stir in the ketchup, vinegar, sherry, remaining soy sauce and the sugar and bring to the boil. Transfer to a dish and keep hot.

To cook the wun tuns, wipe out the wok and add the oil for deep frying. Heat to 190C/375F and add the squares of wun tun dough, a few at a time, cooking them until crisp and golden brown. Place them on a heated serving platter and spoon the duck with sauce into the centre. Serve immediately.

DUCK WITH APRICOTS

SERVES 4

4 duck joints
1 onion
oil
salt and freshly ground black pepper
2 sprigs rosemary
100 g/ 4 oz dried apricots
900 ml/ 1½ pints red wine
sprigs of rosemary to garnish

Trim any excess fat off the duck joints and thinly slice the onion. Grease the wok with a little oil and add the duck joints then fry until well browned. Remove from the wok and drain them on absorbent kitchen paper. Drain all but a thin coating of fat from the wok.

Add the onion to the wok and fry until soft but not browned. Season then add the rosemary. Return the duck to the wok and add the apricots then pour in the wine and bring to the boil. Reduce the heat, put the lid on the wok and simmer for an hour or until the duck is tender.

Adjust the seasoning as necessary, arrange the duck joints on a serving platter and spoon over the sauce. Garnish with a few extra sprigs of rosemary and serve immediately.

Top: *Oriental Duck with Pineapple (page 27)*; bottom: *Wun Tun Duck*

Meat Dishes

There is a dish for every occasion in this chapter – using beef, veal and pork in a selection of tasty combinations. As well as traditional favourites such as Cumberland Pork there are also Chinese dishes such as Pork Wun Tuns.

BEEF STROGANOFF
SERVES 4

This is incredibly quick to cook and ideal both for cooking in, and serving straight from, the wok. Serve with buttered rice or pasta and a fresh green salad.

1 kg/2 lb frying steak
1 onion
100 g/4 oz button mushrooms
50 g/2 oz butter
salt and freshly ground black pepper
4 tablespoons brandy
150 ml/¼ pint soured cream
chopped parsley to garnish

Cut the steak into fine strips. Halve the onion and slice it very thinly, then separate the pieces into fine strips. Slice the mushrooms thinly.

Melt the butter in the wok and add the onion strips and seasoning to taste, then fry until softened. Turn up the heat and make sure that the butter is as hot as it can be without burning, then add the meat and cook very quickly until browned. Stir all the time as the meat cooks to prevent it sticking to the wok. Pour the brandy over the beef and ignite it straightaway. Stir in the mushrooms and heat for a minute, then streak the soured cream through the meat and sprinkle with a little chopped parsley. Serve immediately.

Variations
The stroganoff can be made at less cost using fine strips of lean pork. Lamb is also delicious cooked in this way – choose lean boneless meat from the leg and cut it into fine strips as above.

WIENER SCHNITZEL
SERVES 4

Serve this traditional dish of fried, breaded veal escalopes with sautéed potatoes and broccoli, French beans or a mixed salad.

4 veal escalopes
3 tablespoons plain flour
salt and freshly ground black pepper
1 egg, beaten
100 g/4 oz dry white breadcrumbs
75 g/3 oz butter
Garnish:
2 hard-boiled eggs, chopped
chopped parsley
1 lemon, sliced

Place the escalopes between two sheets of greaseproof paper and beat them out until they are very thin. Mix the flour with plenty of seasoning on a plate and dip the veal in it. Coat the escalopes first in beaten egg and then in the breadcrumbs, pressing them on well.

Melt the butter in the wok and add the veal. Fry until golden on the underside, turning round once so that the coating browns evenly, then turn over and brown the second side. Transfer the cooked veal escalopes to a heated serving platter, pour any pan juices over, and arrange a garnish of chopped hard-boiled egg and chopped parsley round them. Top with slices of lemon and serve immediately.

DEVILLED BEEF FRITTERS

SERVES 4

(Illustrated above)

*450 g / 1 lb lean minced beef or
minced steak
2 tablespoons tomato ketchup
2 teaspoons Dijon mustard
dash of Worcestershire sauce
2 cloves garlic
salt and freshly ground black pepper
½ teaspoon paprika
8 tablespoons self-raising flour
4 eggs
4 tablespoons natural yogurt
1 red pepper
1 green pepper
1 small onion
1 crisp lettuce (cos or iceberg)
oil for frying*
Sauce:
300 ml / ½ pint natural yogurt

Place the mince in a basin and mix in the ketchup, mustard and Worcestershire sauce. Crush the garlic over the meat and mix this in with plenty of salt and pepper and the paprika. Sprinkle the flour, a tablespoon at a time, over the meat mixture and mix in each spoonful so that it is thoroughly and smoothly incorporated. Lightly beat the eggs and pour them over the meat mixture. Gradually mix them in and beat well, then pour in the yogurt and beat the batter thoroughly.

Cut the stalk ends off the peppers and remove all the seeds and pith from inside. Cut the pepper flesh into fine slices. Thinly slice the onion and separate the slices into rings. Separate the lettuce leaves and shred them coarsely.

Heat a little oil in the wok and drop spoonfuls of the batter on to the hot surface – several fritters can be cooked at once on the lower part of the sides of the wok. The fritters should be fairly small. Cook the fritters until they are browned on both sides, then transfer them to absorbent kitchen paper, drain and keep hot.

Add the onion rings and pepper slices to the fat remaining in the pan and stir-fry these for a minute or two, until the onion is just beginning to soften. Arrange the lettuce on a large serving platter and top with the onion and pepper mixture. Arrange the fritters on top and serve, with natural yogurt.

BARBECUED SPARE RIBS

SERVES 4

(Illustrated opposite)
675 g/ 1½ lb pork spare ribs
600 ml/ 1 pint chicken stock
2 tablespoons soy sauce
3 large cloves garlic
½ teaspoon five spice powder
pinch of Chinese red powder
2 tablespoons sesame oil
*2 tablespoons concentrated
tomato purée*
salt
½ medium-sized Chinese cabbage
1 bunch spring onions
2 tablespoons oil

Ask the butcher to separate the spare ribs, or separate them yourself using a meat cleaver. Place the spare ribs in the wok with the stock and stir in the soy sauce. Bring to the boil and put the lid on the wok, then reduce the heat and simmer for 30 minutes, or until the meat is tender.

While the spare ribs are cooking, prepare the sauce. Crush the garlic into a small basin and sprinkle in the five spice powder, and red powder. Stir in the sesame oil and tomato purée and season the mixture with a little salt.

When the spare ribs are cooked, remove them from the wok using a slotted spoon and place them on a plate. Spread the spice mixture over them so that they are all thinly covered – an old pastry brush is useful for this. Set the ribs aside to cool while you prepare the salad ingredients. Shred the Chinese cabbage and trim the spring onions. If you like, the onions may be curled (see Meatballs with Prawns, page 34) or they can be cut into strips.

Remove the stock from the wok – this can be used for soup-making or for preparing a sauce, or it can be frozen for later use, but when it is used it will need diluting with extra water. Rinse and wipe out the wok and rub a little oil round the inside if it is carbon steel. Pour the oil into the wok and place it over a high heat. Add the spare ribs to the smoking oil and cook them quickly, turning once or twice, until crisp and well browned on all sides.

Arrange the prepared salad ingredients on a large serving platter and pile the ribs on top.

Clockwise, from the top: *Prawn Fried Rice (page 61), Barbecued Spare Ribs, Meatballs with Prawns (page 34), Stuffed Chinese Mushrooms (page 44)*

MEATBALLS WITH PRAWNS

SERVES 4

(Illustrated on pages 32–3)

Serve this oriental pork and prawn dish straight from the wok, with steamed rice or cooked egg noodles as accompaniments. Arm your guests with chopsticks and provide small bowls instead of plates.

450 g/1 lb lean minced pork
2 tablespoons fresh breadcrumbs
1 small egg
2 tablespoons soy sauce
3 large dried Chinese mushrooms
2 large spring onions
1 tablespoon light sesame oil
25 g/1 oz flaked almonds
1 teaspoon cornflour
4 tablespoons dry sherry
4 tablespoons chicken stock
100 g/4 oz peeled cooked prawns
Garnish: (optional)
a few spring onions
small bunch of radishes
¼ cucumber

If you are planning on garnishing the dish then prepare the ingredients for the garnish in advance. To make the ends of the spring onions curl, wash and trim off any limp parts. Leave plenty of the green part on the onions, then cut down into these to give fine strips, all attached to the white base. Place the spring onions in a bowl of ice-cold water and set aside in the refrigerator while you are cooking the dish. Spring onion curls can be prepared several hours in advance if you like; they normally take about 45 minutes to curl but this depends on the length of the onions – don't be impatient if they are not ready within an hour!

Trim the radishes. Then, using a sharp pointed knife, make a series of small V-shaped cuts round the centre of each radish, pushing the knife into the middle of each vegetable as you do so. Pull the two halves apart and set aside in a covered dish or piece of cling film. Cut the cucumber diagonally into thin slices and set these aside, again covering them to stop them drying out.

Mix the minced pork with the breadcrumbs, egg and soy sauce, then knead the mixture thoroughly so that it binds together. Shape small spoonfuls of this mixture into balls about the size of walnuts, place them on a plate and set aside.

Place the mushrooms in a small basin and cover with boiling water, then leave them to soak for 10 to 15 minutes, or until they are soft. Chop the spring onions and set aside.

Heat the oil in the wok and add the almonds. Stir-fry for a few minutes until they are lightly browned, then remove from the pan and drain on absorbent kitchen paper. Add the meatballs to the oil remaining in the pan and fry them, turning frequently, until they are browned all over. Take care when turning the meatballs that you do not break them up. While the meatballs are cooking cream the cornflour with the sherry and stock until smooth. Drain and slice the mushrooms.

When all the meatballs are cooked, add the mushrooms and chopped spring onions to the pan and cook for a few minutes. Stir in the prawns, then pour in the cornflour mixture and bring to the boil. Simmer for a few minutes. Arrange the ingredients for the garnish round the meatball mixture, either in the wok or in a heated serving dish, and serve immediately.

VEAL WITH SALAMI

SERVES 4

(Illustrated opposite)

This dish is very rich – serve it with buttered pasta and a tomato salad. A cheaper and equally delicious version can be prepared with chicken instead.

4 veal escalopes
225 g/8 oz Italian salami
225 g/8 oz black olives
1 tablespoon oil
4 tablespoons chopped chives
150 ml/¼ pint soured cream
freshly ground black pepper
paprika to garnish (optional)

Cut the veal and the salami into fine strips and remove the stones from the olives. Heat the oil in the wok, add the veal strips and stir-fry until golden brown. Stir in the olives and salami strips and cook for a minute, then sprinkle over the chopped chives and drizzle the cream over but do not stir it in. Sprinkle with plenty of freshly ground black pepper – this dish should not need any salt because the salami is already highly seasoned – and serve immediately. Garnish with a little paprika, if you like.

ITALIAN VEAL OLIVES

SERVES 4

Veal escalopes, stuffed with Dolcelatte, braised on courgettes and garnished with olives, make this dish ideal dinner party fare. Serve buttered pasta as the only accompaniment.

4 veal escalopes
100 g/4 oz Dolcelatte cheese
2 tablespoons single cream
salt and freshly ground black pepper
1 tablespoon chopped fresh
basil (optional)
4 small courgettes
2 spring onions
2 tablespoons olive oil
2 tablespoons plain flour
4 tablespoons dry white wine
Garnish:
100 g/4 oz black olives
2 tablespoons chopped parsley
2 tomatoes, chopped

Place the escalopes between two sheets of greaseproof paper and beat them out as thinly as possible. Mix the Dolcelatte with the cream, a little salt and freshly ground black pepper, and the basil, if used. Spread this mixture over the veal escalopes, then roll them up neatly to enclose the stuffing. Secure with wooden cocktail sticks and set aside in the refrigerator.

Trim off and discard the ends of the courgettes and cut into slices. Chop the spring onions.

Heat the oil in the wok. Dust the veal rolls with the flour and brown them thoroughly in the hot oil, then, using a slotted spoon, remove them from the pan. Add the courgettes to the oil and toss them lightly, then add the spring onions and wine, and place the veal rolls on top. Cover the wok and simmer for 15 minutes. While the veal is cooking stone and chop the black olives for the garnish.

When cooked, the veal can be transferred to a suitable heated serving dish, with the courgettes arranged around the rolls, or, if your wok is attractive enough, the dish can be served straight from the pan. Sprinkle the black olives, parsley and tomatoes in neat rows to garnish the veal, then serve immediately.

Below: *Veal with Salami*

PESTO PORK

SERVES 4

(Illustrated above)

4 thin pork steaks, cut from the leg
4 large potatoes
450 g/1 lb French beans
oil for frying
salt and freshly ground black pepper
Pesto Sauce:
a large handful of fresh basil
2 large cloves garlic
2 tablespoons pine nuts
2 tablespoons freshly grated
Parmesan cheese
150 ml/¼ pint olive oil

Trim the fat off the pork and set the steaks aside. Cut the potatoes in half and place them on the steaming rack in the wok. Pour in enough water to come up to the level of the rack without touching the potatoes, then bring to the boil and cover the wok. Reduce the heat slightly so that the water simmers quite hard and steam the potatoes for 25 to 30 minutes, or until they are tender. Meanwhile trim the French beans and add them to the steaming rack for the last 10 minutes of the steaming time. Set the cooked vegetables aside, pour the water out of the wok and wipe it dry, greasing it if necessary.

For the pesto sauce, trim any large stalks off the basil and place the leaves in a liquidiser with the garlic, nuts and cheese. Pour in a little of the olive oil and process until smooth, then gradually pour in the remaining oil as the ingredients are processed.

Heat just a little oil in the wok and add the pork, then fry until browned on both sides. Meanwhile, slice the potatoes thickly. When the pork is almost cooked, remove the slices from the wok and lay the potato slices in the pan, seasoning them very lightly. Arrange the French beans on top and lay the pork, overlapping, on top of them. Put the lid on the wok and cook gently until the vegetables are heated through — this should take about 10 minutes.

To serve, pour a little of the pesto sauce down the middle of the pork and offer the rest separately.

PORK WUN TUNS

SERVES 4

Wun tuns are a type of Chinese dumpling and they are made from a dough which is similar to pasta. Once prepared, you can cook wun tuns either by simmering them in liquid or by deep frying them to give crisp, light results. Filled with just a little well-flavoured meat or fish, these frilly-edged dumplings are delicious served with steamed rice.

1 egg, beaten, to seal
the wun tuns
1.15 litres/2 pints Rich
Chicken Stock (page 14)
Wun Tun Dough:
50 g/2 oz plain flour
50 g/2 oz cornflour
2 teaspoons baking powder
pinch of salt
1 egg, lightly beaten
2 tablespoons water
Filling:
100 g/4 oz lean minced pork
2 tablespoons dried shrimps
sesame oil
2 teaspoons soy sauce
½ small onion
Accompaniment:
1 small Chinese cabbage
1 (227-g/8-oz) can bamboo shoots
2 carrots
4 tablespoons dry sherry

First make the dough. Sift the flours, baking powder and salt into a mixing bowl and make a well in the centre. Add the egg and water and mix in the dry ingredients to make a stiff dough. Turn out on to a lightly floured surface and knead thoroughly until very smooth. Work quickly so that the dough does not stick to the work surface and try to avoid using lots of flour. Divide the dough in half and keep the portions covered with cling film while you prepare the filling.

Mix the pork with the shrimps, a few drops of sesame oil and the soy sauce. Chop the onion half very finely and add it to the meat mixture. Stir well to combine all the ingredients.

Back to the dough: take one portion (keep the other covered) and roll it out on a well floured surface until it is very thin. It should form a square of about 25 cm/10 in. The thinner the dough becomes the better the results, but take great care not to rip it when you are rolling it out because it is very difficult to patch up any holes. Trim the edges

and cut out nine small squares. Roll out each of these in turn to give pieces of dough which are roughly 10 cm/4 in square and very thin. Place a little filling (less than a teaspoonful) in the middle of each piece of dough and brush the edges with a little beaten egg. Gather up the dough to enclose the filling completely, sealing it in well but leaving the edges of the dough free. The filled wun tuns should look like small gathered muslin herb bags. Place the filled wun tuns on a large floured board or plate. Repeat with the second portion of dough.

Pour the stock into the wok and bring to the boil, then reduce the heat so that it simmers very gently. Cook the wun tuns in the stock, a few at a time, for 5 minutes. Do not allow the stock to boil too rapidly or the wun tuns may break up and lose their filling. Remove the cooked wun tuns from the stock with a slotted spoon and set aside.

While the wun tuns are cooking shred the Chinese cabbage and slice the drained bamboo shoots. Cut the slices into fine strips. Cut the trimmed carrots into similar-sized strips.

When all the wun tuns are cooked bring the stock to a rapid boil in the open wok and boil hard until it has reduced by half. Add the carrot and bamboo shoot strips to the stock, with the sherry, and boil for a minute. Add the cabbage and reduce the heat, then return the wun tuns to the wok and simmer for 2 minutes to heat through. Serve straightaway.

Variation

Instead of cooking the wun tuns in stock as above why not try deep frying them? Heat 900 ml/1½ pints oil in the wok to 190 C/375 F and add the wun tuns a few at a time. Fry until crisp and golden, then drain on absorbent kitchen paper and arrange on a warmed serving platter.

CUMBERLAND PORK

SERVES 4

(Illustrated opposite)

Pork is an economical meat and, because it is so versatile, it does equally well for the most imaginative dishes or day-to-day ones. Here is a homely dish to serve to the family, accompany it with baked potatoes and a cauliflower gratin or simple buttered vegetables.

1 kg/2 lb lean boneless pork (use
leg, shoulder or trimmed knuckle)
450 g/1 lb pickling onions
2 tablespoons oil
4 tablespoons plain flour
salt and freshly ground black pepper
juice of 2 oranges
300 ml/½ pint red wine
grated rind of 1 orange
100 g/4 oz redcurrant jelly
Garnish:
orange slices
sprigs of watercress

Cut the pork into small cubes and cut any large pickling onions in half. Heat the oil in the wok and add the pork and onions, then cook, stirring frequently, until the meat is browned. Stir in the flour and seasoning and cook for a minute, then pour in the orange juice and wine. Bring to the boil, add the orange rind and redcurrant jelly and stir until the jelly dissolves. Then reduce the heat and simmer for 15 minutes, or until the meat is tender.

To serve, transfer to a heated serving dish and garnish with the orange slices and watercress sprigs.

WOK BEANS

SERVES 4

(Illustrated opposite)

Here is a particularly quick bean-pot recipe made with a couple of cans of beans and some cooked ham. You can, if you like, use frankfurters, smoked Dutch sausage or cold roast pork instead of the ham – in fact, it's just the recipe for using up any tasty leftovers of meat or vegetables.

2 onions
450 g/1 lb cooked ham, in one piece
50 g/2 oz butter
2 cloves garlic
225 g/8 oz sweet corn
2 (425-g/15-oz) cans red kidney beans
1 (397-g/14-oz) can tomatoes
3 tablespoons concentrated
tomato purée
bay leaf
1 teaspoon dried mixed herbs
salt and freshly ground black pepper

Finely chop the onions and cut the ham into cubes. Melt the butter in the wok and crush the garlic into it. Add the onion and fry until it is soft but not browned. Stir in the ham, sweet corn and both cans of beans, with the juice from just one can. Add the tomatoes, tomato purée, bay leaf and herbs and stir well to dissolve the purée. Bring to the boil and add salt and pepper to taste. Reduce the heat and simmer the bean-pot for 3 minutes.

Serve in individual bowls or straight from the wok, and offer a salad of mixed green vegetables and some crusty bread as accompaniments.

Rice & Vegetables

Rice has become a staple food to many in the West and is an enormously useful ingredient to keep in the store cupboard. Rice can be seasoned and flavoured in so many different ways to turn it into a variety of dishes from the plainest to the most elaborate.

Vegetables are best cooked quickly to retain their flavour and vitamins and stir-frying is the ideal way to cook them for slightly crisp results. But there is far more to cooking vegetables in a wok than shredding and tossing as you will find out when you read on!

CREAMED MUSHROOMS AND POTATOES

SERVES 4

I kg/2 lb small new potatoes
50 g/2 oz butter
salt and freshly ground black pepper
I tablespoon plain flour
300 ml/½ pint chicken stock
225 g/8 oz small button mushrooms
300 ml/½ pint single cream
2 tablespoons chopped parsley
to garnish

Scrape the potatoes. Melt the butter in the wok, add the potatoes and seasoning to taste, and cook for a few minutes, turning frequently. Then stir in the flour and gradually pour in the stock. Bring to the boil, reduce the heat and put the lid on the wok. Simmer gently, turning the potatoes occasionally to make sure they cook evenly, for about 20 to 30 minutes, or until the potatoes are tender. (They take longer than normal to cook because they are not covered in boiling water.)

When the potatoes are tender, stir the mushrooms into the sauce and cook for a minute. Then stir in the cream and heat through gently without boiling. Sprinkle the parsley over before serving.

SUMMERTIME POTATOES

SERVES 4

I kg/2 lb small new potatoes
600 ml/I pint chicken stock
350 g/12 oz cooked ham
450 g/I lb peeled cooked prawns
4 spring onions
2 teaspoons chopped mint
2 tablespoons chopped parsley
I tablespoon white wine vinegar
salt and freshly ground black pepper

Scrub or scrape the potatoes and place in the wok. Add the stock and bring to the boil, then cover the wok and reduce the heat so the liquid simmers steadily. Cook for 15 minutes, or until tender.

While the potatoes are cooking cut the ham into small dice and mix with the prawns. Chop the spring onions and mix these with the herbs. Using a slotted spoon, remove the cooked potatoes from the wok. Bring the stock to the boil in the open wok and boil rapidly until it is reduced by half. Add the vinegar to the stock and stir in the ham and prawns. Return the potatoes to the wok and heat through gently for a minute, then add the herbs and spring onions. Stir well to combine all the ingredients and taste and adjust the seasoning.

DOLMADES

SERVES 6

(Illustrated above)

about 30 canned or packeted
vine leaves
1 large onion
1 tablespoon olive oil
2 cloves garlic
salt and freshly ground black pepper
450 g/ 1 lb lean minced lamb
2 teaspoons dried marjoram

Sauce:

300 ml/½ pint chicken stock
1 (397-g/ 14-oz) can tomatoes
2 tablespoons concentrated
tomato purée
300 ml/½ pint red wine
salt and freshly ground black pepper

Rinse and dry the vine leaves and use the largest ones from the can or packet. Finely chop the onion and heat the oil in the wok. Add the onion and crush the garlic into the wok. Sprinkle in seasoning to taste and fry until the onion is soft but not browned. Add the lamb and fry this, breaking up the meat as it cooks, until well browned.

Stir in the marjoram and remove the meat mixture from the wok; set it aside to cool. There is no need to rinse the wok. When the mixture cools, use it to stuff the vine leaves. Place a small spoonful of the filling in the middle of a vine leaf. Fold the sides of the leaf over the meat, then fold the stalk end in towards the middle. Neatly fold the leaf from the stalk end, enclosing the filling in the folds and making sure that the package is secure. Place the leaf in the wok, with the folded side downwards. Continue until all the leaves and meat are used, laying them closely together in the wok and working from the centre outwards in a single layer.

When all the leaves are neatly arranged in the wok, mix the ingredients for the sauce, adding seasoning to taste. Stir until the tomato purée has dissolved and pour the mixture gently into the wok. Make sure that the sauce does not disturb the leaves and allow time for it to seep between the packages. Heat gently until the sauce simmers, then put the lid on the wok and keep the liquid simmering away gently for an hour. By this time the leaves should be tender – test one with a fork or knife.

Serve the dolmades, hot, straight from the wok, or if you wish to serve them cold, transfer them to a serving dish to cool, then chill thoroughly in the refrigerator.

PORCISSON COURGETTES

SERVES 4

This dish is quite substantial enough to serve on its own, with some fresh bread, for lunch or supper. The courgettes cook particularly quickly and the French pork sausage, flavoured with red wine, herbs and spices, adds both flavour and texture. You can also use good-quality salami if you like.

*1 (225-g/8-oz) dried saucisson
(cooked French sausage, flavoured
with garlic, herbs and red wine)
450 g/1 lb courgettes
olive oil
4 tablespoons chopped parsley
2 tablespoons chopped chives
salt and freshly ground black pepper*

Slice the saucisson and trim and slice the courgettes. Grease the wok with just a little oil and heat it over a high heat. Add the saucisson and courgette slices and cook, tossing frequently, until the courgettes are lightly cooked, that is tender but still crisp.

Sprinkle the herbs over, taste and adjust the seasoning if necessary, then serve immediately.

CABBAGE BRAISE

SERVES 4

(Illustrated opposite)

Plain boiled cabbage can be very boring, but this cabbage dish is quite exciting – it's saucy and well flavoured with other vegetables. Serve the crisp wedges of cabbage with the crunchy topping and plenty of warm bread for supper, or omit the topping and serve them to accompany those meat or fish dishes which do not have a sauce.

*1 (1-kg/2-lb) Savoy cabbage
1 onion
2 carrots
2 sticks celery
50 g/2 oz butter
salt and freshly ground black pepper
1 tablespoon plain flour
300 ml/½ pint chicken stock*
Topping: (optional)
*350 g/12 oz lean bacon rashers
3 slices bread
50 g/2 oz butter
2 tablespoons chopped parsley
100 g/4 oz Lancashire or
Caerphilly cheese*

Trim the outside leaves and stalks off the cabbage and cut the cabbage into four wedges. Wash and drain thoroughly. Chop the onion and dice the carrots and celery.

If you are going to serve the topping, then prepare it before cooking the cabbage. Cut the rinds off the bacon and chop the rashers. Cut the crusts off the bread and cut the slices into small cubes. Melt the butter in the wok and fry the cubes of bread in it until golden brown, then remove and drain on absorbent kitchen paper. Add the bacon to the wok and fry until cooked but not crisp. Remove the bacon with a slotted spoon and mix it with the croûtons (fried cubes of bread) and parsley. When cool, stir in the cheese.

To cook the cabbage, melt the butter in the wok and add the onion, carrots, celery and seasoning. Fry until the onion is soft but not browned. Stir in the flour and cook for a minute, then pour in the stock and bring to the boil. Place the wedges of cabbage in the sauce and spoon a little of it over them. Put the lid on the wok and simmer steadily for 25 to 30 minutes, or until the cabbage is cooked to your liking.

Sprinkle the topping (if used) over the cabbage and serve immediately.

Top: *Courgettes with Feta (page 44)*; bottom: *Cabbage Braise*

COURGETTES WITH FETA

SERVES 4

(Illustrated on page 42)

Serve these courgettes as a first course, or as a light lunch or supper dish with warmed pita bread. Alternatively, serve them as an accompaniment to grilled or barbecued lamb chops, or simply fry the chops in your wok first and keep them hot while you quickly prepare the courgettes.

4 large courgettes
175 g/6 oz feta cheese, chilled
4 tablespoons olive oil
1 or 2 cloves garlic
salt and freshly ground black pepper
3 tablespoons chopped fresh basil
1 lemon, cut into wedges, to garnish

Trim the ends off the courgettes and peel the courgettes very lightly – they should be a dark green when a very thin layer of peel is cut off. Cut each courgette lengthways into quarters. Crumble the feta cheese, then return it to the refrigerator because it has to be very cold to complement the fried courgettes.

Heat the oil in the wok and crush the garlic into it; if you are keen on foods which are well flavoured with garlic, then use two cloves. Add the courgettes, season lightly, and fry them quickly until lightly browned. The heat should be high enough to brown the courgettes before they lose their crisp texture. Transfer the courgettes to a heated serving platter and sprinkle the chilled feta cheese over. Top with the basil and pour on the oil from the wok. Arrange the lemon wedges round the courgettes and serve immediately. The combination of flavours and textures in this dish is delicious!

STUFFED CHINESE MUSHROOMS

SERVES 4

(Illustrated on pages 32–3)

16 large dried Chinese mushrooms
450 g/1 lb lean minced pork
2 tablespoons rich soy sauce
sesame oil
generous pinch of ground ginger
16 peeled cooked prawns
Garnish: (optional)
1 small bunch spring onions
a few radishes
1 bunch watercress

Place the mushrooms in a basin and cover them with boiling water, then leave to stand for 30 minutes. Meanwhile, mix the pork with the soy sauce, a few drops of sesame oil and the ginger, making sure that the ingredients are thoroughly combined.

If you wish to garnish the dish, then this would be a good time to trim the spring onions and make them into curls (see Meatballs with Prawns, page 34). Trim the radishes and cut down through them several times, to give small wedges all attached at the base. Place these radish flowers in a bowl of iced water and set in the refrigerator. Trim the watercress and choose eight neat sprigs to set aside.

Drain the soaked mushrooms and divide the filling equally between eight of them, then press the remaining eight mushrooms on top. Press the mushrooms well together between the palms of your hands – hold them over a plate as you do this because a little water may be squeezed out. Place the stuffed mushrooms on a deep plate (one with a rim) or in a shallow dish and stand it on the steaming rack in the wok. Pour in enough water to come up to the level of the rack and bring to the boil, then reduce the heat and simmer rapidly, with the lid on the wok for 20 minutes. Place two peeled prawns on top of each mushroom, re-cover the wok and simmer for a further 5 minutes.

To serve, transfer the mushrooms to a heated serving dish and pour a little of the liquid from the plate over them. Garnish each mushroom with a tiny sprig of watercress placed between the prawns, and arrange the spring onion curls and radish flowers between and around the mushrooms on the plate. Serve immediately.

POTATO AND SALAMI LAYER

SERVES 4

(Illustrated below)

This makes a satisfying and tasty supper dish. You can use any cold sliced meats or sausages instead of the German salami – try other types of mild salami, ham sausage, tongue or hot and spicy Spanish salami, for example.

675 g/ 1½ lb potatoes
2 large onions
50 g/ 2 oz butter
salt and freshly ground black pepper
2 tablespoons chopped mixed
fresh herbs
2 gherkins
2 canned pimientos
225 g/ 8 oz German salami,
thinly sliced

Thinly slice the potatoes and onions, separating the onions into rings. Melt the butter in the wok and fry the onions for a minute. Remove them from the wok and add a layer of potatoes to the pan. Top with some of the onions, plenty of seasoning and a sprinkling of fresh herbs. Continue layering the potatoes and onions with the herbs until they are all used. Put the lid on the wok and cook over medium heat for about 45 minutes, or until the potatoes are cooked. Make sure that the heat is not too fierce or the potatoes at the bottom will overcook.

Meanwhile, slice the gherkins lengthways and cut the pimientos into fine strips. Arrange the salami, gherkins and pimiento strips on top of the potatoes, re-cover the wok and cook for a few minutes more. Serve straight from the wok.

KEDGEREE

SERVES 4

(Illustrated opposite)

Traditionally served for breakfast, kedgeree also makes a delicious lunch or supper dish. Serve this rice and fish mixture straight from the wok and offer a fresh green salad and some Granary bread as the only accompaniments.

1 large onion
2 tablespoons oil
225 g/8 oz long-grain rice
½ teaspoon turmeric
600 ml/1 pint chicken stock
450 g/1 lb smoked haddock
4 hard-boiled eggs
2 tablespoons chopped parsley
salt and freshly ground black pepper

Chop the onion. Heat the oil in the wok, add the onion and cook, stirring frequently, until soft but not browned. Add the rice and fry this for a few minutes, turning it in the oil until it is lightly browned. Stir in the turmeric and gradually add the stock. Take care not to burn yourself in the gush of steam which rises as the liquid first enters the wok.

Bring to the boil, then lower the heat slightly and put the lid on the wok. Simmer for 10 minutes. Lay the fish on top of the half-cooked rice, re-cover the wok and continue to cook for a further 10 minutes. Use a fish slice to lift the fish on to a plate, then flake the flesh and discard any bones and the skin.

Quarter the hard-boiled eggs and stir these into the wok with the fish. Sprinkle over the parsley and season with salt and plenty of black pepper. Toss lightly and serve immediately.

PAELLA

SERVES 4

(Illustrated opposite)

The wok is ideal for cooking paella because small pans will not hold all the ingredients necessary for this dish. Serve the paella straight from the wok with a crisp, mixed green salad.

350 g/12 oz lean boneless pork
1 large onion
2 tablespoons olive oil
4 chicken drumsticks
2 large cloves garlic
1 red pepper
1 green pepper
225 g/8 oz long-grain rice
¼ teaspoon powdered saffron
salt and freshly ground black pepper
450 ml/¾ pint chicken stock
150 ml/¼ pint full-bodied red wine
225 g/8 oz peeled cooked prawns
225 g/8 oz cooked mussels (fresh,
frozen or canned in brine, but not
pickled)
225 g/8 oz frozen peas
cooked whole shellfish to garnish

Cut the pork into small cubes and chop the onion. Heat the oil in the wok, add the chicken drumsticks and brown them all over. Add the pork, onion and crushed garlic, cover the wok and cook for 15 minutes. Check occasionally to make sure that the pork is not sticking to the pan.

Meanwhile, cut off and discard the stalk ends of the peppers, remove their seeds and pith, then slice the flesh into neat rings. Add these to the meats in the wok together with the rice and saffron. Cook, stirring, for a few minutes, then add seasoning to taste and pour in the stock and wine. Bring to the boil, reduce the heat and put the lid on the wok. Simmer for a further 15 minutes, then add the prawns, mussels and peas; do not stir these into the rice but let them cook on top. Re-cover the wok and cook for 15 minutes more. Toss the ingredients lightly and serve immediately, garnished with cooked whole shellfish of your choice.

SIMPLE CHOP SUEY

SERVES 4

This quick stir-fry vegetable dish is an excellent side dish for serving with fried Chinese dishes like Barbecued Spare Ribs (page 32).

1 small onion
2 carrots
1 (227-g/8-oz) can bamboo shoots
350 g/12 oz bean sprouts
1 tablespoon sunflower oil
1 small clove garlic
3–4 tablespoons soy sauce

Halve the onion, then cut it into very thin slices and separate the slices into strips. Trim the carrots and cut them into very fine strips, and do the same with the drained bamboo shoots. Pick over the bean sprouts, removing any which are slightly brown and as many of the green pods as possible.

Heat the oil in the wok and crush the garlic into it, then add the onion and carrots. Stir-fry for a few minutes, or until the onion has softened slightly. Stir in the bamboo shoots and cook for a minute, then add the bean sprouts and stir-fry for another minute before adding soy sauce to taste. Serve immediately – the bean sprouts should still be very crunchy.

OKRA WITH TOMATOES

SERVES 4

(Illustrated right)
Serve this lightly spiced vegetable mixture as an accompaniment to curries, or with simple grilled, fried or barbecued meats.

450 g/1 lb okra
450 g/1 lb tomatoes
1 small onion
25 g/1 oz butter and
2 tablespoons oil
4 green cardamoms
salt and freshly ground black pepper
1 teaspoon garam masala
2 tablespoons chopped fresh
coriander leaves

Trim off and discard the ends of the okra and slice them into chunks. Place the tomatoes in a large bowl and pour in enough boiling water to cover them. Allow to stand for 30 seconds to a minute, then drain and peel them. Thinly slice the onion and quarter the peeled tomatoes.

Melt the butter and oil in the wok and add the cardamoms. Fry these for a few seconds, then add the onion and a little salt and pepper and cook until soft but not browned. Add the okra and tomatoes and cook for a few minutes, stirring the vegetables frequently. The okra should be tender but take care not to overcook them because then they become slimy and unpleasant in texture.

As soon as the vegetables are cooked, sprinkle on the garam masala and chopped coriander and serve immediately.

LAMB PILAF

SERVES 4

(Illustrated above)

675 g/ 1½ lb lean boneless lamb
1 large onion
1 large green pepper
2 tablespoons olive oil
25 g/ 1 oz flaked almonds
2 cloves garlic
225 g/ 8 oz long-grain rice
bay leaf
1 stick cinnamon
600 ml/ 1 pint robust red wine
50 g/ 2 oz black olives
salt and freshly ground black pepper
4 tablespoons chopped fresh
coriander
Garnish:
1 lemon
paprika

Cut the lamb into neat, fairly small cubes and chop the onion. Cut the stalk end off the green pepper, then remove all the seeds and pith and chop the flesh. Heat the oil in the wok and add the flaked almonds. Cook until they are lightly browned, then remove them from the wok with a slotted spoon and drain on absorbent kitchen paper.

Add the lamb to the oil remaining in the wok and crush the garlic over it. Fry, turning frequently, until well browned on all sides. Add the onion, green pepper and rice and continue frying until the grains of rice are transparent and lightly browned. Add the bay leaf and cinnamon stick and carefully pour in the wine. Take care not to burn your arm in the gush of steam which rises as the wine hits the hot wok. Bring to the boil, put the lid on the wok and reduce the heat so that the pilaf simmers gently. Cook for 10 minutes.

While the pilaf is cooking, stone the olives and add these to the rice mixture after the 10 minutes' cooking time. Continue cooking for a further 5 minutes.

Cut the lemon for the garnish into eight wedges. When the pilaf is cooked, taste and adjust the seasoning if necessary, and stir in the coriander. To serve, arrange the lemon wedges around the rice, either in the wok or in a separate heated serving dish, and sprinkle a little paprika over each piece of lemon. Top with the fried almonds and serve.

VEGETABLE RISOTTO

SERVES 4

(Illustrated opposite)

4 sticks celery
1 green pepper
100 g/4 oz carrots
2 large onions
2 tablespoons olive oil
2 cloves garlic
225 g/8 oz walnut pieces
175 g/6 oz long-grain rice
salt and freshly ground black pepper
600 ml/1 pint chicken or
vegetable stock
450 g/1 lb tomatoes
100 g/4 oz black olives
100 g/4 oz sweet corn
100 g/4 oz frozen peas
4 tablespoons chopped fresh herbs

Slice the celery. Cut off and discard the stalk end of the pepper and remove all the seeds and pith from the inside, then roughly chop the flesh. Slice the carrots and roughly chop the onions.

Heat the oil in the wok, crush the garlic into it and add the walnuts. Fry, stirring frequently, until the nuts are lightly browned, then remove them from the wok using a slotted spoon and drain on absorbent kitchen paper. Add the prepared vegetables to the oil remaining in the wok and cook until slightly softened. Stir in the rice and seasoning to taste, then pour in the stock and bring to the boil. Put the lid on the wok and reduce the heat so that the risotto simmers gently. Cook for 10 minutes.

While the rice is cooking, place the tomatoes in a bowl and pour on enough boiling water to cover them completely. Leave to stand for 30 seconds to a minute, then drain, peel and quarter the tomatoes. Stone the olives and mix them with the tomatoes.

When the rice has cooked for 10 minutes, stir in the sweet corn and peas, place the tomatoes and olives on top (do not stir them in) and put the lid back on the wok. Continue simmering the risotto for a further 5 minutes, by which time all the stock should have been absorbed and the rice should be cooked. Before serving, stir in the tomatoes, olives, nuts and herbs. Serve straight from the wok if you like, with a creamy salad.

Clockwise, from the top: *Crunchy Tofu (page 59) with sauce accompaniments on far right, Vegetable Risotto with courgette salad, Falafal (page 59)*

EGG-FRIED RICE WITH SAUSAGE

SERVES 4

Chinese sausages are dried, spiced pork sausages containing pieces of meat and, sometimes, liver. They have a slightly sweet taste and should be cooked in moist dishes or steamed before being added to vegetable dishes. They are delicious and add an excellent flavour to steamed rice if they are balanced over the dish in which the rice is cooked, and then sliced diagonally to serve. Serve this rice dish with simple stir-fried meat and vegetables, or serve it just on its own because it is quite substantial and well flavoured.

2 tablespoons oil
225 g/8 oz long-grain rice
4 large dried Chinese mushrooms
600 ml/1 pint chicken stock
8 Chinese sausages
1 bunch spring onions
2 eggs
1 (227-g/8-oz) can water chestnuts

Heat half the oil in the wok and add the rice, then fry this until the grains are transparent and lightly browned. Meanwhile, place the mushrooms in a small basin and cover with boiling water. Allow to soak for 5 minutes.

When the rice is browned, carefully pour the stock into the wok. As the liquid hits the hot pan clouds of steam will rise, so take care not to burn your arm. When the steam has subsided, stand the steaming rack in the wok over the rice and place the sausages on this rack. Bring the stock back to the boil, then reduce the heat so that it simmers steadily. Drain the mushrooms and stand them on the rack next to the sausages. Put the lid on the wok and simmer for 15 minutes, or until the rice has absorbed all the stock.

Meanwhile, trim the spring onions and cut them diagonally into strips. Lightly beat the eggs and set aside. Drain and slice the water chestnuts.

When the rice is cooked, remove the steaming rack from the wok and slice the sausages diagonally. Slice the mushrooms and add these to the sausages, set aside and keep hot. Push the rice up the sides of the wok to make a well in the middle. Add the remaining oil to this space and fry the sliced water chestnuts for a minute, then remove them with a slotted spoon and add them to the sausages and mushrooms. Pour the egg into the wok and cook, stirring, until just beginning to set. Mix with the rice and cook for a few seconds.

Remove the wok from the heat and arrange the sausage mixture on top. Sprinkle the spring onions over and serve immediately. Alternatively the rice mixture can be transferred to a serving dish and the sausage mixture added as above.

FRUIT PULLAO

SERVES 4

This is a particularly splendid pullao, with apricots, raisins and almonds added. To emphasise the scented basmati rice add a few drops of rose water.

225 g/8 oz basmati rice
1 large onion
225 g/8 oz dried apricots
50 g/2 oz raisins
75 g/3 oz butter
50 g/2 oz flaked almonds
2 sticks of cinnamon
bay leaf
2 cloves
6 coriander seeds
2 green cardamoms
salt and freshly ground black pepper
600 ml/1 pint water

Rinse the rice thoroughly under plenty of cold running water, until the water runs clear, then set the rice aside to drain. Chop the onion and the apricots and mix both with the raisins.

Melt the butter in the wok and add the almonds. Fry until lightly browned, then remove with a slotted spoon. Add the onion mixture to the wok and fry over medium heat, stirring continuously, until the onion is just soft. Add the spices and continue cooking for a minute, then stir in salt and pepper to taste and the rice. Cook for another minute, then add the water. Bring to the boil and reduce the heat so that the rice barely simmers, then put the lid on the wok and cook for about 25 minutes. By this time all the liquid should have been absorbed and the rice should be cooked.

To serve, fork up the rice and sprinkle the almonds over the top.

JAMBALAYA

SERVES 4

(Illustrated above)

Jambalaya is a spicy mixture of meats (ham and chicken), prawns and rice, with peppers and chillies too. All the ingredients are cooked together, making this dish particularly easy to prepare and serve, and it's great fun to eat it straight from the wok. So give your guests small bowls, and keep the food hot by placing the wok over a plate warmer or on a fondue burner turned down very low. Make the Fruity Green Salad (overleaf) and have some warm pita bread or French bread around in case anyone is ravenous!

450 g| 1 lb gammon, in one piece
450 g| 1 lb chicken meat
1 large onion
1 green pepper
1 red pepper
4 green chillies
50 g| 2 oz butter
2 cloves garlic
salt and freshly ground black pepper
225 g| 8 oz long-grain rice
½ teaspoon turmeric

600 ml| 1 pint chicken stock
dash of Tabasco sauce
225 g| 8 oz peeled cooked prawns
paprika

Cut the gammon into bite-sized cubes and cut the chicken into similar-sized pieces. Chop the onion and cut the stalk ends off the peppers. Remove all the seeds and pith from inside the peppers and chop the flesh. Cut the stalk ends off the chillies and remove all their seeds, then slice them thinly.

Melt the butter in the wok and crush the garlic into it. Add the gammon, chicken and salt and pepper to taste, then fry until browned on all sides. Add the onion, peppers and chillies and continue cooking until the onion has softened slightly. Stir in the rice and turmeric, reduce the heat, then pour in the stock and add the Tabasco. Stir well and bring to the boil, cover the wok and reduce the heat so that the jambalaya simmers gently. Cook for 10 minutes before adding the prawns, then cook for a further 5 to 10 minutes, or until the rice is cooked and most of the stock has been absorbed to leave a moist dish. Sprinkle with a little paprika before serving.

Lunch & Supper Dishes

Here are recipes for light meals that can be quickly made in the wok. Some of them, such as the samosas, can be used as an accompaniment to a main meal. To show the versatility of the wok, there is even an easy recipe for pizza which has a crisp base and a moist topping – delicious!

NOODLES WITH CUCUMBER

SERVES 4

*350 g/12 oz chow mein noodles
(thin Chinese egg noodles)
1.15 litres/2 pints boiling water
pinch of salt
½ cucumber
3 green chillies
1 bunch spring onions
2 tablespoons oil
1 clove garlic*

Place the noodles in the wok and pour the boiling water over them. Add a pinch of salt and bring to the boil, then put the lid on the wok and reduce the heat so that the water simmers rapidly. Cook for 3 to 5 minutes.

While the noodles are cooking, finely peel the cucumber and cut it into matchstick strips. Cut the tops off the chillies and remove their seeds, then finely slice the green part. Trim and chop the spring onions.

Drain the noodles when they are cooked and heat the oil in the wok. Add the cucumber, chillies and spring onions and cook, stirring, for a minute. Crush the garlic into the wok and stir for another minute, then add the cooked noodles. Toss well to combine the ingredients and put the lid on the wok. Cook over gentle heat for 2 to 3 minutes, or until the noodles are hot. Serve immediately.

FRUITY GREEN SALAD

SERVES 4

*1 endive or crisp lettuce
1 bunch spring onions
¼ cucumber
2 sticks celery
4 ripe peaches
juice of 1 lemon
2 slices onion
4 tablespoons olive oil
1 teaspoon prepared mild mustard
salt and freshly ground black pepper*

Wash and dry the endive or lettuce then shred roughly. Place in a salad bowl. Trim and chop the spring onions, lightly peel and dice the cucumber and add both to the salad. Trim the celery and cut it lengthways into very fine strips, then into 5-cm/2-in lengths. Place in a bowl of iced water and leave for 15 minutes, then drain and dry on absorbent kitchen paper before sprinkling over the salad.

Place the peaches in a bowl and pour on boiling water to cover. Leave to stand for 1 minute, then drain and peel the fruit. Halve the peaches and remove their stones, then cut the flesh into slices and sprinkle the lemon juice over them. Add to the salad, with a few slices of onion if liked.

Mix the olive oil with the remaining lemon juice, mustard and seasoning to taste, then sprinkle this dressing over the salad and serve.

PRAWN CURRY

SERVES 4

(Illustrated below)

This is excellent but rather expensive, so if you feel that you cannot stretch to serving this as a main course dish for more than two, try making half the quantity and serving it on a few crisp lettuce leaves as a starter.

> 1 large onion
> 2 stalks lemon grass or pared rind of ½ lemon
> 3 green chillies
> 25 g/1 oz fresh root ginger
> 2 cloves garlic
> 50 g/2 oz butter
> 4 green cardamoms
> 1 tablespoon garam masala
> salt and freshly ground black pepper
> 1 kg/2 lb peeled cooked prawns
> chopped fresh coriander leaves to garnish

Finely chop the onion and cut each stalk of lemon grass into two or three pieces. Cut the stalk ends off the chillies and scoop out and discard all the seeds. Finely chop the green part and mix it with the onion and lemon grass or lemon rind. Grate the ginger and crush the garlic, and mix these together.

Melt the butter in the wok and add the onion mixture, then fry until the onion is soft but not browned. Add the ginger and garlic and cook for a further 2 to 3 minutes before stirring in the cardamoms and garam masala. Add salt and pepper to taste and continue to cook, stirring to prevent the mixture from sticking to the wok, until the cardamoms give off their appetising aroma.

Now add the prawns and toss them in the spices and juices. Put the lid on the wok and cook over a gentle heat for 3 to 5 minutes. The heat should be low enough to allow the prawns to heat through and absorb the flavour from the other ingredients without overcooking. To serve, transfer the curry to a heated serving dish or simply leave it in the wok. Sprinkle a generous amount of chopped coriander over at the last minute.

WOK PIZZA

SERVES 1 to 4

(Illustrated opposite)

Here is a very quick and easy recipe for a pizza, and it's not a second rate attempt at imitating the real thing either! The base is made of bread mix, which is cooked on the hot surface of the wok to give a crisp light result similar to that achieved when a pizza is cooked in a very hot oven. The topping is moist and well flavoured, and there is a whole list of alternative topping suggestions given below.

150 g/5 oz bread mix
about 100 ml/4 fl oz lukewarm water
Topping:
1 large onion
3 tablespoons olive oil
2 cloves garlic
1 teaspoon dried oregano
½ teaspoon dried thyme
1 teaspoon marjoram
salt and freshly ground black pepper
4 tablespoons concentrated tomato purée
175 g/6 oz mozzarella cheese
1 (50-g/1¾-oz) can anchovies
a few black olives

The quantity of bread mix you need to use is about half of a standard packet size. Make it up with the water, having read the packet instructions first to check the quantities – for this recipe you have to add just a little extra water to give a soft dough. Knead the dough for about 10 minutes, again reading the instructions on the packet. Set aside while the topping is being prepared.

Finely chop the onion. Heat the oil in the wok and add the onion, then crush the garlic into it. Cook until soft but not browned, then add the herbs and seasoning and remove from the heat. Transfer the topping to a basin and stir in the tomato purée. Slice the cheese and halve the anchovy fillets, reserving the oil from the can to pour over the pizza if you like. Remove the stones from a few black olives.

Roll out the dough to give a 25-cm/10-in round. Heat the wok – it should still contain some oil from the filling, or at least it should be well greased. Carefully lift the pizza base into the wok; use a spatula to do this to make sure that there will be no creases in the dough. Reduce the heat so that the bread will not brown and cook for a few minutes, until the underside is starting to cook and form a crust. Turn the dough over and spread the tomato mixture on top. Lay the slices of cheese evenly over

the pizza and arrange the anchovy fillets and olives in a lattice pattern on top.

Put the lid on the wok and increase the heat so that the base of the pizza cooks crisply and bubbles slightly. The pizza should be cooked through in about 5 minutes. During cooking, carefully lift the sides of the dough and make sure that it is not burning in the middle underneath. You can slide the pizza round the wok slightly to ensure that it cooks evenly. Serve immediately, sliding the pizza out on to a warmed serving platter and cutting it into portions if you wish to serve more than one.

Variations

Retain the tomato base and try any of the following topping ideas. The ingredients should be sprinkled over the tomato mixture before you put the cheese on top.

Seafood Pizza Sprinkle over 100 g/4 oz peeled cooked prawns and add 1 (198-g/7-oz) can tuna fish, flaked with its oil.

Salami Pizza Arrange 50 g/2 oz thinly sliced Italian salami over the tomato mixture. Omit the anchovies and use stuffed green olives, sliced, instead of the black ones.

Pepper Pizza Sauté 2 thinly sliced red or green peppers in the oil and remove them from the wok before adding the onion and tomato mixture. Sprinkle the peppers over the tomato topping before adding the cheese. Omit the anchovies and top the pizza with 50 g/2 oz cooked ham, cut into fine strips, with the olives.

Bacon Pizza Chop 175 g/6 oz rindless streaky bacon and fry it in the wok before preparing the tomato topping. Use only 50 g/2 oz mozzarella and cut it into small cubes. Mix the fried bacon with 1 (396-g/14-oz) can artichoke hearts, drained, and the anchovies and olives. Top the tomato mixture with the bacon mixture and dot the cubes of cheese over the top.

PLAICE GOUJONS WITH VEGETABLES

SERVES 4

(Illustrated below)

8 plaice fillets
3 tablespoons plain flour
salt and freshly ground black pepper
I egg, beaten
75 g/3 oz fine dry breadcrumbs
3 sticks celery
100 g/4 oz carrots
I red pepper
I small onion
2 tablespoons oil

Sauce:

2 tablespoons chopped capers
2 tablespoons chopped parsley
I teaspoon grated lemon rind
150 ml/¼ pint mayonnaise
150 ml/¼ pint soured cream
salt and freshly ground black pepper

Skin the plaice fillets (see Paupiettes Florentine, page 18) and cut the flesh into fine strips. Mix the flour with the seasoning on a plate or in a polythene bag. Coat the fish strips in the seasoned flour, either by rolling them on the plate or by shaking them in the bag. Dip the fish first in the beaten egg, then in the breadcrumbs, pressing them on well. Place the strips in the refrigerator while you prepare the vegetables.

Finely slice the celery and carrots. Cut the stalk end off the pepper and remove the seeds and pith from inside, then cut the flesh into thin slices. Halve and slice the onion.

Heat the oil in the wok, add the fish strips and fry them, turning once or twice, until golden and crisp. Drain on absorbent kitchen paper and set aside to keep hot. Add the prepared vegetables to the fat remaining in the wok and stir-fry them until they are just tender. Arrange the vegetables on a heated serving dish, or leave them in the wok and place the fish goujons on top.

To make the sauce, mix the capers, parsley and lemon rind into the mayonnaise. Stir in the soured cream and season to taste. Serve the fish and vegetables, with the sauce handed separately in a small bowl.

CRUNCHY TOFU

SERVES 4

(Illustrated on page 50)

450 g/ 1 lb tofu
4 tablespoons plain flour
freshly grated nutmeg
salt and freshly ground black pepper
1 egg
75–100 g/ 3–4 oz dry white
breadcrumbs
900 ml/ 1½ pints oil for deep frying
Sauce:
1 large clove garlic
2 tablespoons concentrated
tomato purée
4 tablespoons chopped fresh herbs
150 ml/¼ pint natural yogurt
150 ml/¼ pint double cream,
lightly whipped
salt and freshly ground black pepper
Garnish:
watercress sprigs
lemon wedges

Cut the tofu into slices. Mix the flour with grated nutmeg to taste and plenty of salt and pepper, then use it to coat the tofu. Lightly beat the egg, then dip the slices of tofu in the beaten egg, coat them thoroughly in the breadcrumbs and chill.

To prepare the sauce, crush the garlic into the tomato purée in a small bowl, then stir in the herbs, yogurt, cream and seasoning to taste. Chill until required.

Pour the oil for deep frying into the wok and heat it to 190C/375F. Add the tofu and fry, a few pieces at a time, until crisp and golden. Remove with a slotted spoon and drain on absorbent kitchen paper. Keep hot.

When all the tofu is cooked, arrange the slices on a heated serving dish and garnish with watercress sprigs and lemon wedges. Serve immediately, with the sauce handed separately.

FALAFAL

SERVES 4

(Illustrated on page 50)

225 g/ 8 oz dried chick peas
salt and freshly ground black pepper
½ teaspoon ground coriander
2 tablespoons chopped mixed parsley
and thyme
2 cloves garlic
900 ml/ 1½ pints oil for deep frying
Salad:
1 crisp lettuce (for example, iceberg
or cos)
1 small red onion
½ cucumber
100 g/ 4 oz black olives
4 tomatoes
Dressing:
50 g/ 2 oz crunchy peanut butter
4 tablespoons olive oil
grated rind and juice of 1 lemon
dash of Tabasco sauce
salt and freshly ground black pepper

Soak the chick peas overnight in cold water to cover. Next day, drain them and grind them finely in a liquidiser. Transfer the ground mixture to a bowl and stir in seasoning to taste, the coriander, herbs and crushed garlic. Mix the ingredients thoroughly, then take small spoonfuls of the mixture and shape into balls about the size of walnuts. Knead thoroughly to make the mixture bind together.

To make the salad, shred the lettuce and place it in a large bowl. Thinly slice the onion and divide the slices into rings, then thinly slice the cucumber. Mix both into the lettuce. Stone the olives and add them to the salad. Lastly, place the tomatoes in a large heatproof bowl and add boiling water to cover. Leave for 30 seconds to a minute, then drain and peel the tomatoes. Cut them into quarters or eighths and add them to the salad, then toss the salad lightly and arrange it on a serving platter. Mix all the ingredients for the dressing and add seasoning to taste. Pour the dressing over the salad.

Heat the oil for deep frying in the wok until it reaches 190C/375F, then add the chick pea balls, a few at a time, and fry until golden brown. Drain on absorbent kitchen paper and pile the hot falafal on top of the salad. Serve immediately, with plenty of warm pita bread.

BEEF CHOW MEIN

SERVES 4

(Illustrated opposite)
This dish makes a satisfying meal in itself; serve a cucumber and chicory salad as the only accompaniment.

450 g/1 lb frying steak
1 small onion
1 stick celery
1 carrot
4 large dried Chinese mushrooms
1 large clove garlic
2 tablespoons soy sauce
salt
350 g/12 oz chow mein noodles (thin Chinese egg noodles)
2 tablespoons light sesame oil
150 ml/¼ pint beef stock
4 tablespoons dry sherry

Cut the meat into fine strips. Halve and thinly slice the onion and cut the celery into short, fine strips. Cut the carrot into fine strips. Place the mushrooms in a small basin and cover with boiling water, then leave to stand for about 15 minutes, or until they are soft enough to slice. Crush the garlic and mix it with the soy sauce, then pour this over the meat in a basin and use your fingers to rub the sauce well into the strips of meat. Set aside.

Bring 1.15 litres/2 pints water to the boil in the wok and season it lightly with a little salt. Add the noodles and put the lid on the wok, then simmer for 5 minutes. Drain and set aside the noodles and wipe out the wok with absorbent kitchen paper. Drain and slice the mushrooms.

Heat the oil in the wok, add the steak and stir-fry for about 5 minutes, or until the meat is browned. Then add the onion, celery and carrot and cook for a minute. Stir in the mushrooms, stock and sherry and bring to the boil, then add the cooked noodles and toss them with the other ingredients. Cook for 2 to 3 minutes, then serve.

Variation

The chow mein can be served in small Oriental-style pancakes if you like. To make the pancakes, sift 225 g/8 oz plain flour into a bowl and add a pinch of salt. Stir in 150 ml/¼ pint boiling water and knead the ingredients together to make a smooth dough. Divide into 12 pieces and roll each into a 15-cm/6-in circle. Brush half the circles with a little sesame oil and press a second circle on each so that they are sandwiched in pairs.

Heat a little oil in the wok and cook the pancake pairs individually over a moderate heat until browned lightly on both sides. Remove from the pan, separate the pancakes and keep hot on a plate over a saucepan of simmering water.

To serve, fill the pancakes with a little chow mein, then offer shredded spring onions and bottled hoisin sauce as accompaniments.

PRAWN FRIED RICE

SERVES 4

(Illustrated on pages 32–3)
Fried rice is quite easy to prepare but it is important first to cook the rice sufficiently in the oil until the grains are transparent; that way the finished dish will always have a good flavour.

1 onion
3 tablespoons oil
1 clove garlic
225 g/8 oz long-grain rice
salt and freshly ground black pepper
600 ml/1 pint chicken stock
225 g/8 oz frozen peas
225 g/8 oz peeled cooked prawns

Chop the onion. Heat the oil in the wok and crush the garlic into it. Add the onion and cook until softened but not brown. Add the rice and stir-fry until the grains are transparent and lightly browned. Add seasoning to taste and carefully pour in the stock – take care because a cloud of steam will rise from the wok and this may burn your hand or arm if it is in the way. Bring to the boil, reduce the heat and put the lid on the wok, then simmer gently for 15 minutes.

When the rice has absorbed most of the stock stir in the peas and prawns and continue cooking for a further 5 minutes; make sure that the rice does not overcook and burn at this stage. Serve straight from the wok or spoon the fried rice into a heated serving bowl.

Variations

Add deseeded and chopped red and green peppers, diced carrots and celery or chopped chillies when you fry the rice. If you wish to add frozen sweet corn or other frozen mixed vegetables, stir them into the rice 5 minutes before the end of the cooking time. Add chopped nuts or herbs when the rice is cooked.

CRISPY NOODLES WITH MUSHROOMS AND HAM

SERVES 4

These crunchy noodles are delicious with stir-fried cooked ham and soaked Chinese mushrooms. You can boil the noodles in advance if you wish, ready for frying at the last minute.

salt and freshly ground black pepper
350 g/12 oz chow mein noodles (thin Chinese egg noodles)
6 large dried Chinese mushrooms
225 g/8 oz cooked ham
1 bunch spring onions
2 tablespoons oil
50 g/2 oz butter

Pour 1.15 litres/2 pints water into the wok and add a little salt, then bring to the boil and add the noodles. Put the lid on the wok and simmer for about 5 minutes; when cooked the noodles should be tender but not sticky. Drain the noodles and place them on a plate, patting them into a round shape.

Place the mushrooms in a basin and pour in enough boiling water to cover them completely, then leave to soak for 15 minutes. Drain and slice. Cut the ham into shreds and trim and shred the spring onions.

Heat the oil and butter together in the wok and add the mushrooms, ham and spring onions. Cook for a few minutes, then remove with a slotted spoon and set aside. Slide the noodles into the wok and cook over a high heat until they are golden and crisp underneath, then turn them over and cook the second side in the same way. Sprinkle the ham mixture over the noodles and serve immediately.

CHINESE-STYLE TOFU

SERVES 4

Tofu, or bean curd, is made from ground, soaked soya beans – it is a sort of soya cheese. To eat on its own it is tasteless and has a texture which is reminiscent of a chilled custard, but it is high in food value (protein) and because it lacks any distinctive taste it can be seasoned and flavoured in any number of dishes. You can buy tofu in health food stores and Chinese supermarkets. Traditionally used in Chinese cooking, it is also used in lots of vegetarian dishes. Serve Chinese-style Tofu with spicy rice or meat dishes, or serve it on its own as a starter.

1 (227-g/8-oz) can bamboo shoots
175 g/6 oz mangetout peas
350 g/12 oz tofu
4 tablespoons oil
1 clove garlic
4 tablespoons soy sauce
2 tablespoons roasted sesame seeds

Slice, then shred the drained bamboo shoots. Trim the ends of the mangetout peas and string them if necessary. Cut the tofu into 5-mm/$\frac{1}{4}$-in thick slices.

Heat the oil in the wok and crush the garlic into it. Add the tofu and fry the slices until crisp and golden, then remove them from the wok with a slotted spoon and drain on absorbent kitchen paper. Add the mangetout peas and bamboo shoots to the wok, and stir-fry for 5 minutes, then sprinkle the soy sauce and sesame seeds over them. Return the tofu to the wok and cook for a further minute before serving.

PIPÉRADE

SERVES 4

(Illustrated above)

This is a dish of fried peppers and onions with scrambled eggs – it is ideal for a quick lunch or supper dish, or it can be served as a first course. Crisp bread and butter – French or Granary – is the best accompaniment.

2 green peppers
2 red peppers
2 onions
1 large clove garlic
50 g/2 oz butter
4 large eggs
salt and freshly ground black pepper

Cut off and discard the stalk ends of the peppers and remove all the seeds and pith from inside. Slice the pepper shells into very thin rings. Slice the onions thinly and separate the slices into rings. Crush the garlic into the wok and add the butter. Melt over a medium heat, then add the peppers and onions and fry fairly slowly until they are well cooked and soft.

Whisk the eggs with plenty of seasoning and add them to the wok, stirring well. Cook, stirring all the time, until the eggs are just beginning to set, then stop stirring and continue cooking over a low heat until the eggs are set to taste – they should be creamy rather than solid. Serve immediately, straight from the wok if you like.

Mixed Soup Pot

SERVES 4

(Illustrated opposite)

*900 ml/ 1½ pints Rich
Chicken Stock (page 14)
1 small Chinese cabbage
1 bunch spring onions
1 red pepper
150 ml/¼ pint dry sherry
about 300 ml/½ pint water
salt and freshly ground black pepper*
To cook at the table:
*1 quantity Pork Wun Tuns (page 37)
a selection of raw seafood, chicken,
beef and Chinese sausages*

First prepare the stock according to the recipe instructions. Pour it into the wok and add the reserved, chopped, cooked chicken meat.

Shred the Chinese cabbage and chop the spring onions, then add these to the stock. Cut the stalk end off the red pepper and remove all the seeds and pith from inside, then halve the flesh and cut it into fine strips. Add these to the wok. Pour in the sherry and water – you may need to add more water at the end of the meal; it depends on how much liquid evaporates during cooking. Add seasoning to taste.

Now prepare the ingredients for cooking at the table, slicing them into thin, neat pieces. You do not have to present a wide variety of foods – if you like you can have just one sort of fish and some meat. It is important whenever you present raw foods at the table to make sure they are attractively garnished.

Prepare the wun tun dough and filling according to the recipe instructions. Place a teaspoon or so of filling in the centre of each wun tun skin. Bring opposite corners together over the filling and seal the edges firmly. Fold the remaining two corners towards each other, to form a shape resembling a mitre, and seal.

Bring the soup in the wok to the boil on the cooker hob. Have ready the burner on a heatproof mat on the table. Boil the soup for 2 minutes, then take the wok to the table. Arrange all the dishes around the wok and encourage your guests to help themselves. Most of the foods will cook in 1 or 2 minutes; the wun tuns will take 5 minutes – these can be dropped into the soup a few at a time.

When all the foods are eaten put any remaining pieces into the soup and add a little extra water if you like. Heat through for a few minutes, then ladle the soup into bowls and eat it to round off the meal.

NEW POTATO CURRY

SERVES 4

(Illustrated opposite)

2 large onions
1 kg/2 lb small new potatoes
50 g/2 oz fresh root ginger
2 cloves garlic
50 g/2 oz butter
2 bay leaves
1 stick cinnamon
2 teaspoons fennel seeds
3 green cardamoms
1 teaspoon turmeric
600 ml/1 pint water
salt and freshly ground black pepper
300 ml/½ pint natural yogurt
Garnish:
chilli powder to taste
chopped fresh coriander leaves

Finely chop the onions and scrape the potatoes (you can use old potatoes if you like but the flavour is not quite as good). Grate the ginger and crush the garlic and mix both together. Melt the butter in the wok and add the onion, ginger mixture, bay leaves, broken cinnamon stick, fennel seeds, cardamoms and turmeric. Fry, stirring continuously, until the onion is soft but not browned. Stir in the potatoes, pour in the water and add salt and pepper to taste, then bring to the boil and cover the wok. Simmer steadily for 10 minutes, then uncover the wok and cook fairly rapidly for about 10 minutes, or until most of the water has evaporated.

Pour the yogurt over the potatoes and heat through fairly gently, to avoid curdling the sauce. Sprinkle chilli powder to taste and coriander over before serving the curry with any of the accompaniments suggested below.

Accompaniments

Peeled cooked prawns, sprinkled with a little grated lemon rind and chilli powder.
Bombay ducks (strongly flavoured dried fish), grilled until crisp and served with lemon wedges.
Chopped cooked chicken, sprinkled with toasted flaked almonds and chopped chillies.
Peeled green and red peppers, chopped and sprinkled with a little crushed garlic and oil.
Wedges of cucumber, sprinkled with a pinch each of ground cloves and chilli powder.
Quartered tomatoes, sprinkled with thinly sliced onion rings.

GOBHI MASALA

SERVES 4

(Illustrated opposite)

1 large cauliflower
2 onions
50 g/2 oz fresh root ginger
2 cloves garlic
4 green chillies
bay leaf
4 green cardamoms
1 clove
1 stick cinnamon
1 tablespoon mustard seeds
2 tablespoons poppy seeds
½ teaspoon turmeric
450 g/1 lb tomatoes
3 tablespoons concentrated
tomato purée
150 ml/¼ pint water
50 g/2 oz butter
300 ml/½ pint natural yogurt

Place the cauliflower on the steaming rack in the wok and add water to come up to the level of the rack but without touching the cauliflower. Bring to the boil and put the lid on the wok, then reduce the heat and simmer steadily for 15 minutes.

Meanwhile, chop the onions, grate the ginger and crush the garlic. Cut the stalk ends off the chillies and remove the seeds and pith, then chop the green part finely. In a small, heavy-based frying pan, roast the bay leaf with the cardamoms, clove, broken cinnamon stick and mustard and poppy seeds over a low heat until they give off a strong aroma. Do not overcook the spices or they will taste very bitter. Remove the spices from the pan and cool slightly, then grind them to a powder in a liquidiser. Add half the chopped onion and the ginger and garlic, then process to form a paste. Mix in the turmeric.

Peel the tomatoes then cut them into quarters. Stir the tomato purée into the water and set aside.

Remove the cauliflower and pour away the water. Wipe and grease the wok, add the butter and melt it over a medium heat. Add the remaining chopped onion and the chillies and cook, stirring frequently, until soft but not browned. Stir in the paste and cook, stirring, for about 5 minutes.

Pour the dissolved tomato purée into the wok and add the tomato quarters. Bring to the boil, simmer for 5 minutes, then stir in the yogurt and add the cauliflower, in florets. Stir well to coat the florets. Cover and simmer gently for 15 minutes.

SAMOSAS

MAKES 8

(Illustrated opposite)

These are small Indian pasties filled with either meat or vegetables. They are meant to be a snack, but they are also ideal for serving as a starter or as one of the side dishes in an Indian meal.

1 onion
2 green chillies
15 g/½ oz fresh root ginger
1 tablespoon oil
2 cloves garlic
½ teaspoon mustard seeds
225 g/8 oz lean minced beef
2 tablespoons chopped fresh
coriander leaves (optional)
salt and freshly ground black pepper
beaten egg
Dough:
100 g/4 oz plain flour
pinch of salt
1 egg
3 tablespoons oil
1 tablespoon water

Finely chop the onion, deseed and chop the chillies and finely chop the ginger. Heat the oil in the wok and add the onion and ginger, then fry until the onion is soft but not browned. Stir in the chillies, crushed garlic, mustard seeds and beef, and cook, breaking up the meat as it cooks, until evenly browned. Add the coriander and seasoning to taste, then remove this filling from the wok and wipe out the pan.

To make the dough, sift the flour into a bowl with the salt. Make a well in the centre and add the lightly beaten egg, oil and water. Stir these ingredients together in the middle of the flour until they are lightly mixed, then gradually stir in the flour and knead together to make a firm dough. Knead thoroughly on a lightly floured board until very smooth, then divide the dough into eight evenly sized portions.

Roll out each portion of dough to give a round measuring about 15 cm/6 in. in diameter. Take a circle of dough in the palm of your hand and make a pleat in it to take up about a quarter of the circle. Lift the dough off the palm and hold it between your thumb and forefinger, with your thumb and forefinger formed into an almost closed circle; the pleated side of the dough should be over your thumb and the main part of the dough should hang down into your hand to form a cone. Spoon some of the mixture into the cone and brush the edges with a little beaten egg, then pinch the edges together firmly, to seal in the filling. When the samosa is laid flat it should now be almost triangular in shape. Repeat with the remaining dough and filling.

Wipe out the wok and pour in the oil for deep frying. Heat the oil to 190C/375F and fry the samosas, one or two at a time, until they are crisp and golden. Drain on absorbent kitchen paper and serve hot or cold.

POPCORN

MAKES a 1.15-litre/2-pint bowlful

(Illustrated opposite)

2 tablespoons oil
50 g/2 oz popping corn
75 g/3 oz butter
50 g/2 oz sugar

Heat the oil in the wok until it is just beginning to smoke. Slide in all the corn at once and put the lid on the wok straightaway. Using oven gloves to hold the wok and its lid, shake the pan occasionally and cook over a medium-high heat until the popping stops.

When the corn has stopped popping open the wok and add the butter, in knobs, then sprinkle in the sugar. Cool the popcorn, with the lid on and shaking the wok all the time, for 2 to 3 minutes. Open the wok and toss the corn in the buttery caramel, then turn the corn into a bowl and pour in any caramel from the wok. Leave for a minute or two because it will still be very hot, then serve.

Variations

The popcorn can also be served as a savoury snack. Cook it as above and when the corn has stopped popping sprinkle it with chopped spring onions, grated cheese, chopped ham, fried chopped bacon, butter with herbs and salt and pepper, or any other combination of ingredients which takes your fancy. Try having a popcorn party and cook the corn while your guests look on!

Puddings

Here is a limited selection of puddings which can be cooked to advantage in the wok. This chapter emphasises the surprising uses to which a wok can be put – for example, it acts as a marvellous steamer with perfect results.

CHINESE-STYLE FRUIT FRITTERS

SERVES 4

Crisp, batter-coated pieces of apple and banana, coated with caramel and sprinkled with roasted sesame seeds, are mouth-watering. Remember that they are also quite filling so, if you're planning to serve them for dessert, make a light main course.

2 bananas
2 cooking apples
100 g/4 oz self-raising flour
150 ml/¼ pint water
2 eggs, separated
900 ml/1½ pints oil for deep frying
2 tablespoons roasted sesame seeds
Caramel:
100 g/4 oz sugar
100 ml/4 fl oz water

Cut the bananas into chunks. Peel, core and quarter the apples, then cut them into chunks.

Sift the flour into a mixing bowl and make a well in the centre. Pour in the water and add the egg yolks, then beat in the flour to make a smooth batter. Whisk the egg whites until very stiff, then fold them into the batter.

Pour the oil for deep frying into the wok and heat it to 190C/375F. Dip the pieces of fruit, a few at a time, into the batter and then cook them in the hot oil until crisp and golden. Remove with a slotted spoon and drain on absorbent kitchen paper. When you are about three-quarters of the way through cooking the fritters, place the sugar for the caramel in a saucepan with the water and bring to the boil, stirring occasionally until the sugar dissolves. Boil the sugar syrup hard until it reaches a light caramel

– do not stir it at all once it starts boiling.

By now you should have finished cooking all the fritters and they should be draining on absorbent kitchen paper. Place them slightly apart on a large, lightly oiled platter and drizzle the caramel over them, turning them over with a fork to coat the other side in a little caramel. Sprinkle with the sesame seeds and serve immediately.

COCONUT-COATED BANANAS

SERVES 4

8 small bananas
1 egg white
75 g/3 oz desiccated coconut
butter for frying
grated rind and juice of 2 oranges
4 tablespoons rum
3 tablespoons brown sugar

Dip the bananas in the egg white then coat thoroughly in the coconut. Set to one side to allow the coating to harden slightly.

Melt a little butter in the wok and add the bananas, then fry until golden on the underside. Turn the bananas carefully to avoid breaking off the coconut, then cook until golden on the second side. Remove from the wok and arrange the bananas on a heated serving dish.

Add the remaining ingredients to the butter remaining in the wok and bring to the boil. Boil for 1 minute then pour over the bananas and serve immediately.

JAM ROLY-POLY

SERVES 4

(Illustrated above)

This is an economical winter pudding for hungry people. Serve it with a custard sauce.

*225 g/8 oz self-raising flour
100 g/4 oz shredded beef suet
pinch of salt
scant 150 ml/¼ pint water
350 g/12 oz strawberry jam
caster sugar to decorate*

Sift the flour into a mixing bowl and add the suet and salt. Stir in sufficient water to make a soft dough, then knead it very lightly and roll it out on a floured surface to give a rectangle measuring about 25 x 20 cm/10 x 8 in. Spread the jam over the centre of the dough, leaving a 1-cm/½-in border all round the edge. Fold this dough border over the jam, brush the edges with a little water, then roll up the dough to enclose the jam. Place the roly-poly on a large piece of greased foil and wrap it up, sealing the edges thoroughly to make sure that no steam enters during cooking.

Place the steaming rack in the wok and lay the package on it. Pour in enough water to come up to the rack without touching the foil. Bring the water to the boil, cover the wok and simmer for 1½ hours, adding more water as necessary.

To serve, open the foil, slide the roly-poly on to a warm serving plate and sprinkle it with a little caster sugar. Serve immediately.

Variation

The jam used in this recipe can be changed from the traditional strawberry jam to raspberry, apricot, blackcurrant or red cherry.

CRÈME CARAMEL

SERVES 4

(Illustrated opposite)

Make these individual custards the day before you plan to serve them and chill them thoroughly overnight. Although the caramel has to be prepared in a saucepan, steaming the custards in the wok saves putting the oven on, and they are less likely to curdle cooked this way.

100 g/4 oz sugar
100 ml/4 fl oz water
2 small eggs
2 scant tablespoons sugar
350 ml/12 fl oz milk
vanilla pod

Place the 100 g/4 oz of sugar and the water in a saucepan and bring to the boil, stirring occasionally until the sugar dissolves. Boil hard, without stirring at all, until the syrup caramelises – this should take 3 or 4 minutes. As soon as the syrup starts to change colour watch it very carefully, then when it is a light caramel colour remove the pan from the heat and roll the syrup round the sides of the saucepan – it will continue cooking in the heat of the pan. When it becomes a dark caramel colour divide it between four ovenproof ramekin dishes and roll the caramel round the sides of each. Hold the dishes with a tea towel as you do this because they become very hot. Set aside.

Whisk the eggs with the tablespoons of sugar – I find 1 tablespoon of sugar is just too little and, for my liking, 2 tablespoons give a custard that is just too sweet, so adust the quantity to taste.

Pour the milk into a saucepan and add the broken vanilla pod, then bring the milk to the boil and set it aside to cool until hand hot. Remove the vanilla pod and pour the milk on to the eggs, whisk lightly, then strain the custard into the ramekins. Cover each with a square of buttered foil, pinching the edge firmly under the rim of the dish to prevent steam from entering. Stand the dishes on the steaming rack in the wok and pour in enough water to come up to the level of the rack. Bring the water to the boil, then reduce the heat so that the water simmers and put the lid on the wok. Simmer for 20 minutes, or until the custards are set, then remove the dishes and take off the foil. (The time it takes for the custards to set will depend upon how fast the water simmers – about 20 minutes should be right, but check them after 15 minutes.) Allow to cool, then chill overnight or for several hours. Turn out and serve with a jug of single cream.

PEAR AND PLUM COMPOTE

SERVES 4

(Illustrated opposite)

Served with clotted or whipped cream this fruit dessert is quite luscious.

4 large ripe pears
450 g/1 lb plums
300 ml/½ pint rosé wine
100 g/4 oz sugar
grated rind of 1 small orange

Peel, quarter and core the pears, then place the fruit in the wok. Halve and stone the plums and add them to the pears. Pour in the wine, then stir in the sugar and orange rind.

Bring to the boil, then reduce the heat so that the syrup simmers gently and cook for 10 minutes. Serve immediately, or chill thoroughly and serve cold.

CARAMELISED PINEAPPLE

SERVES 4

1 large pineapple
50 g/2 oz butter
4 tablespoons demerara sugar
4 tablespoons kirsch
2 tablespoons chopped pistachio nuts
2 tablespoons chopped maraschino cherries

Trim the leaves off the pineapple and cut off the stalk end. Using a sharp knife, cut off all the peel and remove the spines. Slice the fruit fairly thickly and remove the hard core from each slice.

Melt the butter in the wok and add the pineapple slices, frying both sides for a few seconds. Sprinkle the sugar over and turn the slices of fruit, then cook until the sugar caramelises, turning the fruit once again. As soon as the sugar is lightly browned, turn off the heat and pour in the kirsch. Sprinkle on the nuts and cherries and serve.

BLACKCURRANT PUDDING

SERVES 6

(Illustrated above)

This recipe is excellent for turning a small quantity of blackcurrants into a deliciously well-flavoured pudding. Serve it with whipped cream or vanilla ice cream.

450 g/1 lb fresh or
frozen blackcurrants
100 g/4 oz butter or margarine
175 g/6 oz caster sugar
2 eggs
175 g/6 oz self-raising flour
1 teaspoon baking powder
caster sugar to decorate (optional)

Top and tail fresh blackcurrants, rinse and drain them and set aside; do not defrost frozen fruit. Cream the butter or margarine with the sugar until very soft and pale, then gradually beat in the eggs. Sift the flour and baking powder together, then gently fold into the pudding mixture using a metal spoon.

Place about one-third of the blackcurrants in the base of a deep buttered 15-cm/6-in soufflé dish. Fold the remaining fruit into the pudding mixture and spoon this over the currants in the dish. Spread the mixture evenly and wrap the whole dish in plenty of foil, making sure that it is sharply folded to seal all the edges and prevent any steam from entering and making the pudding soggy during cooking.

Place the steaming rack in the wok and pour in enough water to come up to the top of it. Stand the dish on the rack and bring the water to the boil. Put the lid on the wok and boil steadily for about 2 hours. Check to make sure that the liquid does not boil dry during the cooking time and top it up with more boiling water if necessary.

To serve, lift the dish from the wok and remove the foil, then turn the pudding out on to a heated serving dish. Sprinkle with a little caster sugar before serving, if liked.

UPSIDE-DOWN CAKE

SERVES 6

(Illustrated below)

The wok is very useful for steaming sweet puddings, and here is an impressive yet economical dessert for cool winter days. Serve this pudding with a custard sauce or whipped cream.

4 canned pineapple rings
6 glacé cherries
100 g / 4 oz butter
100 g / 4 oz caster sugar
grated rind of 1 large orange
2 eggs
100 g / 4 oz self-raising flour

Arrange three of the pineapple rings in the base of a buttered 15-cm/6-in soufflé dish. Cut the remaining pineapple ring into thirds and arrange in pieces between the rings in the dish. Place the cherries in any gaps between the rings and place one in the centre.

Cream the butter with the sugar and orange rind until pale and soft. Gradually beat in the eggs with just a little of the flour, then use a metal spoon to fold in the remaining flour. Spoon the mixture into the dish, taking care not to disturb the arrangement of the fruit in the base. Wrap the dish completely in foil, making sure that it is securely folded to prevent any steam from entering. Stand the dish on the steaming rack in the wok and pour in enough water to come up to the base of the dish. Put the lid on the wok and bring the water to the boil, then boil steadily for 1½ hours. Check to make sure that the wok does not boil dry during cooking and add more boiling water if necessary.

When cooked, carefully lift the dish from the wok and remove the foil wrapping, then turn the pudding out on to a heated serving plate and serve hot.

Index